BORO'S B[illegible]T

The [illegible] and fans' fabulous fifty

Sponsored by AYRESOME LEISURE

Dave Allan
Adrian Bevington
Mark Hooper

Juniper Publishing
Liverpool

First Published in Great Britain by
Juniper Publishing
3, Sandy Lane, Melling, Liverpool L31 1EJ
1997

Photographic Acknowledgements: Allsport, ASP, Blades, Football Archive, Arthur Foreman, Highland Studios

ISBN 0-9528622-1-2

Typesetting and origination by: P's & Q's Ltd., Unit 10, Gibraltar Row, King Edward Industrial Estate, Liverpool L3 7HJ.

Printed and bound by: Albion Graphics, Old Connolly Complex, Kirkby Bank Road, Knowsley Industrial Park North, Kirkby, Merseyside, L33 7SY

Contents

The Players and Managers who voted

The authors are very grateful to the following Boro players and managers past and present for their valuable contributions which have made this book such a unique publication:

Malcolm Allison
Stan Anderson
Viv Anderson
Mike Angus
Bob Appleby
David Armstrong
Billy Ashcroft
Ian Bailey
Ian Baird
Michael Barron
Peter Beagrie
Mikkel Beck
Harry Bell
Ray Bilcliff
Ralph Birkett
Clayton Blackmore
Tom Blenkinsopp
Stuart Boam
Mark Burke
Mick Burns
Geoff Butler
Andrew Campbell
Jack Charlton
Brian Clough
Terry Cochrane
Simon Coleman
Alan Comfort
Colin Cooper
Terry Cooper
Neil Cox
John Craggs
Pat Cuff
Stan Cummins
Peter Davenport
Billy Day
Ronnie Dicks
Emerson
Micky Fenton
Gianluca Festa
Arthur Fitzsimons
Jan Fjortoft
Curtis Fleming
Alan Foggon
Chris Freestone
Bill Gates
Gary Gill
Dean Glover
Gary Hamilton
George Hardwick
Graeme Hedley
John Hendrie
John Hickton
Craig Hignett
David Hodgson
Billy Horner
Arthur Horsfield
Ian Ironside
Jack Jennings
Ian Johnson
Peter Johnson
Gordon Jones
Juninho
Chris Kamara
Alan Kernaghan
Paul Kerr
Vladimir Kinder
Lennie Lawrence
Brian Laws
Craig Liddle
Willie Maddren
John Mahoney
Don Masson
Tony McAndrew
Alex McCrae
Hugh McIlmoyle
Mick McNeil
Alan Miller
David Mills
Nicky Mohan
Alan Moore
Chris Morris
Tony Mowbray
Bobby Murdoch
Alan Murray
Robbie Mustoe
Irving Nattrass
John Neal
Mel Nurse
Keith O'Halloran
Kelham O'Hanlon
John O'Rourke
Heine Otto
Gary Pallister
Alan Peacock
Stephen Pears
Nigel Pearson
Bryan Phillips
Jimmy Phillips
Jim Platt
Jamie Pollock
Mark Proctor
Trevor Putney
Fabrizio Ravanelli
Bruce Rioch
Stuart Ripley
Ben Roberts
Dicky Robinson
Bryan Robson
Dicky Rooks
Colin Ross
Trevor Senior
Harold Shepherdson
Bernie Slaven
Malcolm Smith
Graeme Souness
Frank Spraggon
Johnny Spuhler
Phil Stamp
Archie Stephens
Nobby Stiles
Derek Stonehouse
Mark Summerbell
Andrew Todd
Colin Todd
Lee Turnbull
Rolando Ugolini
Steve Vickers
Geoff Walker
Gary Walsh
Charlie Wayman
Phil Whelan
Willie Whigham
Derek Whyte
Paul Wilkinson
Alf Wood
Darren Wood
Tommy Wright
Ray Yeoman

Introduction

Boro's Best is a unique book in the world of football publishing. Never before has a club polled so many of its players and managers, past and present, to name their team's all-time greatest stars.

It took months of research, phone calls and interviews to track down well over 100 former Middlesbrough players and to record their views, along with more than 20 current players, on their Boro favourites. The result is an enchanting, thought-provoking collage of the best players ever to have pulled on the famous red and white shirt.

Each player was asked to name in order the players they rated as the five best they had ever seen in a Boro shirt, whilst giving their view on just what made the recipients of their votes so special. Players chosen as a players' number one choice received five points, second placed players received four points and so on, down to a fifth choice player receiving one point. All of the points were then amalgamated to give each player a total score. Their overall position in the top 50 was based on this score. The same format was used for votes from the fans, who were also asked to name their top five Boro stars.

One of the most intriguing results of the book is the comparison between the players' top 50 and the top 50 chosen by the fans. As many as 13 players who appeared in the players' list did not receive enough votes to appear in the fans' top 50 and vice versa.

And whilst the overall winners on the top 50's were undoubtedly world class international stars, it is incredible to think that the majority of players in both lists failed to win a full cap during their time with Boro. As many as 30 of the players' 50 remained uncapped during their time with the club – 22 of them failing to win a cap throughout their careers and the other eight earning international recognition either before or after their spells on Teesside.

The majority of the players' list – 28 in all are English but the Scots (12), Brazilians (2), Northern Irish (2), Southern Irish (1), Welsh (1), Dutch (1), Italians (1) and Australians (1) are also represented, together with a certain Scotsman-cum-Irishman, Bernie Slaven! Curiously, the Scots suffer most in the fans' list as only five players from North of the border achieved a top 50 placing from those on the terraces. The supporters spread their votes across the globe among English (29), Scots (5), Northern Irish (3), Brazilians (2), Italians (2), Southern Irish (1) Welsh (1), Dutch (1), Danes (1), Norwegians (1), Australians (1), Germans (1), Jamaicans (1) and, again, the same Scotsman who joined up with the Republic of Ireland ranks.

Finally, whilst the players distributed their votes evenly among forwards (15), midfielders (16), defenders (15) and goalkeepers (4), the fans, unsurprisingly, were more biased towards the goalscorers, choosing 22 forwards among their top 50, along with 11 midfielders, 14 defenders and three goalkeepers.

But in this day and age of spiralling transfer fees it is worth noting that, whilst big money buys like Juninho, Ravanelli, Emerson and Barmby all received plenty of votes, 23 of the players' top 50 cost the club a grand total of absolutely nothing! Who says there's no bargains to be found?

With reference to career records included in Boro's Best, please note that all cup details include FA Cup, League Cup (in all its guises), ZDS Cup, Full Members Cup, Anglo-Italian Cup, Anglo-Scottish Cup, Texaco Cup, Simod Cup and Freight/Rover Trophy, together with all promotion play-off games. League totals refer to league games only and do not include play-off games.

Enjoy the book

Dave Allan, Adrian Bevington and
Mark Hooper
Co Authors.

Part One

The Players' Choice

The Players' Top 50

The top Boro stars of all-time, as chosen by those who have played or managed the club.

1	Graeme Souness
2	Juninho
3	Gary Pallister
4	Wilf Mannion
5	Willie Maddren
6	Brian Clough
7	Tony Mowbray
8	Stephen Pears
9	Bernie Slaven
10	David Armstrong
11	Emerson
12	John Hickton
13	George Harwick
14	Fabrizio Ravanelli
15	Bobby Murdoch
16	John Hendrie
17	Bill Harris
18	Craig Johnston
19	Bryan Robson
20	Bob Baxter
21	Robbie Mustoe
22	Micky Fenton
23	Alan Peacock
24	Stuart Boam
25	Dicky Robinson
26	Gary Hamilton
27	George Camsell
28	Stuart Ripley
29	Alex McCrae
30	Terry Cooper
31	Rolando Ugolini
32	Jim Platt
33	Ian Gibson
34	David Hodgson
35	Mark Proctor
36	Nick Barmby
37	Colin Cooper
38	Heine Otto
39	Willie Fernie
40	Tony McAndrew
41	Jimmy Gordon
42	Gordon Jones
43	Curtis Fleming
44	Dave Cumming
45	Eric McMordie
46	Mick McNeil
47	John O'Rourke
48	Hugh McIlmoyle
49	Cyril Knowles
50	John Craggs

Foreword

by Graeme Souness

The players' number one player

Over the years there have been many great Boro players and I am delighted to have been chosen by my peers as their number one. I always said they knew a good player when they saw one up there on Teesside!

I was too young to have seen players like Wilf Mannion, George Hardwick and Brian Clough play, but I know how highly they were regarded, so it's quite an accolade for me to finish above them in the poll.

In my time at Ayresome Park during the 1970's, we had some fine players in the side. I voted for Willie Maddren as my number one. I believe he was a wonderful player who should have been capped by England. In the present team it's good to see players such as Emerson, who looks to be an outstanding midfield player, carrying on the tradition.

In many ways, my time at Middlesbrough was my happiest in football because it was where I matured both as a person and as a professional footballer. When I was at Tottenham Hotspur like a lot of 15-year-olds, I thought I knew everything, but the down-to-earth attitude of the people of Middlesbrough and the club helped me keep my feet firmly on the ground.

My managers at the Boro, Jack Charlton and John Neal, also influenced me. You always learn from the managers you work with and they gave me the good start which laid the foundation for what I have achieved in the game. I only wish that Jack had pushed the boat out a bit to buy one or two quality players because I certainly believe we would have won a major trophy. We did win the Second Division championship but I thought we should have gone on from there.

With all the notable players that are listed in the top fifty I still find it amazing that Boro had never reached a major cup final until 1997.

In conclusion, I would like to take this opportunity to wish Middlesbrough Football Club and its supporters all the best in the future and, once again, I convey my appreciation to all the players and fans who voted for me.

Graeme SOUNESS

" He was the most complete midfield player "

Born: Edinburgh 06-05-53

The launchpad for the battling Scot's illustrious career came when he moved to Boro after failing to make an impression with Tottenham. Souness had represented his country at schoolboy and youth levels and signed on with Spurs as an apprentice in 1969, turning professional in the following year. But after three years at the club, Spurs decided that the future international star was surplus to requirements and Souness was allowed to leave.

Boro manager Stan Anderson swooped for the midfielder in December 1972 and brought him to Ayresome Park for a fee of £32,000. Souness joined the club in the Second Division but in the following season, with Jack Charlton now at the Boro helm, he tasted double success with a call-up to the Scotland under-23 side and a Second Division championship medal. Once in the top flight, Souness graduated to the full Scotland national side and earned the first of 54 caps in a 3-0 win against East Germany in October 1974.

In January 1978, Souness was sold to Liverpool for a club record fee of £352,000. In seven successful seasons at the club, Souness won three European Cups and five Championships and was captain of club and country. He was sold to Sampdoria in June 1984 and then returned to Britain as player-manager at Glasgow Rangers in 1986.

After guiding Rangers to the Premier Division title in his first season and to three further Championships, he returned to Liverpool. Success came in the shape of the 1992 FA Cup but Souness had to contend with a triple heart bypass and failed to bring the title back to Anfield, parting company with the club in 1994. He was then recruited by Turkish giants Galatasaray where he won the Turkish cup. But in 1996, Souness was once again back in England as manager of Southampton.

Graeme Souness tops the poll picked by his peers.

BORO RECORD 1972-78

Season	Div	League App	League Gls	Cup App	Cup Gls	Total App	Total Gls
1972/73	2	11	0	1	0	12	0
1973/74	1	34(1)	7	4	0	38(1)	7
1974/75	1	38	7	11	0	49	7
1975/76	1	34(1)	3	12	2	46(1)	5
1976/77	1	38	2	9	3	47	5
1977/78	1	19	3	3	0	22	3
Total		**174(2)**	**22**	**40**	**5**	**214(2)**	**27**

Scotland: 54 caps (3 with Boro) 3 gls.

Souness was admired by fans and players alike for his combination of artistry and tenacity.

Why Souness is the best!

"He learnt a lot from Bobby Murdoch in his younger days and turned out to be a class player. He was strong and a good passer and also had that nasty streak you need to be a great midfield player. He was also a great example for the younger lads at the club."
Tony McAndrew.

"You've got to respect Souness for the way he overcame rejection and failure at Spurs to become probably the best midfielder in Europe. He did that by first becoming a great player during his years with Middlesbrough and then stepping up on that with Liverpool. He had everything a midfielder could wish for."
Viv Anderson.

"A great player. Graeme was so determined with a great will to win which went along with his abilities to pass the ball. He could create things but also destroy what the other team was doing. He could look after himself and if the players around needed any protection we looked to Graeme. He held the team together in midfield."
David Armstrong.

MY TOP 5
Graeme Souness

1 Willie Maddren
2 David Armstrong
3 Terry Cooper
4 Craig Johnston
5 Emerson

"He was the most complete midfield player I ever saw. Rarely do we see someone with skill, vision and the ruthlessness. He could win the ball and distribute it. He was a world class player."
Malcolm Smith.

"I never played with him but against him for Newcastle and Blackpool and he was a class player. He was great passer of the ball and had that competitive nature which instilled confidence in those around him. Of all the Middlesbrough players I played with or against he shone through with the ability you needed to be a top international."
Mick Burns.

MY TOP 5
Ian Baird

1 Graeme Souness
2 Juninho
3 Tony Mowbray
4 Gary Pallister
5 Bernie Slaven

"Souness thought winner, wanted to be a winner and was a winner. He made most of us look like mere mortals alongside him in the Boro team of the mid-70s. He really was international class. He had skill, tenacity and was a great passer."
Alf Wood.

"Graeme was always a good player. Some people forget about how good he was at Middlesbrough because he achieved so much at Liverpool. I don't think I played against him when he was at Ayresome Park but he was very well thought of."
Bryan Robson.

"I only ever see Souness on the television like everybody else but he was a tough tackler and also had terrific vision. They are quite rare qualities to go together. More often than not midfielders are either creative or hard and you can make it as a top player with either of these qualities. But to have both makes you exceptional."
Alan Comfort.

"Alongside Bryan Robson, they were the two best midfield players of the modern game. At Middlesbrough he had the ability and the potential and turned out to be a world class player. His contribution at Middlesbrough established the club in the First Division."
David Mills.

Jack Charlton, pictured at Redcar Races, is credited with turning Souness into a top class player.

WIth fierce determination on his face, Souness rifles in a shot against Leeds in 1975.

"It was early days for his career and he became more established at Liverpool but I think it all began at Ayresome Park. He was a playmaker and an orchestrator, a good passer of the ball and a very good tackler. He was also a good leader of people and a winner as well as a team player - superb qualities for a professional footballer."
Bruce Rioch.

"Even when he first came to Middlesbrough and was establishing himself in the side, he was one we looked up to. Whoever you were playing, even against the top sides, he would be in there battling. He went on to achieve what he promised with Liverpool and Scotland. He was self-motivated and always wanted to play higher and he earned it by his performances on the field."
Ian Bailey.

MY TOP 5
Alan Miller

1 Graeme Souness
2 John Hendrie
3 Bernie Slaven
4 Steve Pears
5 Robbie Mustoe

"He came to Middlesbrough as a kid when I was just leaving but under Jack Charlton's guidance, he went on to become one of the great players. At first he was doing fancy flicks but Jack got his mind on the game and it was the springboard for his career."
Nobby Stiles.

"He was an all-round player. Most clubs we played were frightened of him, not just because of the physical side of his game but also because of his ability on the ball."
Stuart Boam.

MY TOP 5
Stan Cummins

1 Graeme Souness
2 Willie Maddren
3 Terry Cooper
4 Bobby Murdoch
5 John Hickton

"Graeme was the best player I ever played with. He was a classy player and a fierce competitor. He never lost the ball, you could give him it even while he was marked very tightly and he wouldn't give it away. It was as if he was always thinking about how he was going to use it before he received it."
Peter Johnson.

"He had everything. He was in midfield where all the action was and was a great passer and influence on the team. He could also score goals. When he came from Tottenham, he was a bit of a Jack the lad but Jack Charlton got hold of him and calmed him down. He was a little bit arrogant but not in a nasty way."
John Craggs.

"He was a raw youngster when he first came but he got better and became even better after leaving Middlesbrough. He always had the potential, was very competitive, a good passer of the ball and scored important goals."
Jim Platt.

Graeme Souness

His honour-laden career at Liverpool saw Souness reach the heights but it all began at Ayresome Park. Here he is pictured with former Boro and Liverpool team-mate David Hodgson.

"I have a lot of respect for the career Graeme had. He enjoyed success everywhere he played. He had a good attitude, he was hard but he was also quite fair and his achievements speak for themselves."
Jan Fjortoft.

"When you look at a midfield player today, Graeme Souness is everything you would want him to be. He could dictate a whole game, he had a great desire and aggression allied with a great first touch and passing ability."
Tony Mowbray.

"To me Graeme Souness had everything a midfielder or inside forward should have. He had aggression which won him tackles, passing ability, he could strike a ball and he led by example. Basically he was a winner and you could tell from the moment he arrived from Tottenham even when we were playing five-a-sides in training. He was young with a lot of confidence and a good team player."
Frank Spraggon.

"He was just class. He was a bit rough when he first came but we knocked the edges off him and he got better and better."
Alan Foggon.

During his playing days at Liverpool, Graeme Souness was nicknamed 'Champagne Charlie'. Manager Bob Paisley made the classic remark: "Graeme does not toss a coin at a match - he flips a Gold American Express card."

"He had the edge on everyone else. He had style, he was a hard man and all the young pro's at the club respected him more than anyone when he was there. He had an aura about him, a presence that always had him marked down as a captain."
Graham Hedley.

"He had everything you would look for in a player today. He had the desire and the will to win, the ability to inspire his team-mates and a great range of passing. He was one of the complete players."
Alan Murray.

"I remember seeing him as a child and being impressed but when I came to Middlesbrough I realised how well everybody thought of him around the town. He was revered by everyone. He seemed to have an aura about him as a player and always seemed to win the midfield battles. Every side needs a player like him."
Alan Miller.

"First and foremost he was Scottish! He was class, the best midfielder of his era who was a general on the field."
John Hendrie.

"I played with him and he was a very good player. He was as strong as a bull, had good vision and had a touch of confidence bordering on arrogance."
Pat Cuff.

"When he first arrived at Middlesbrough, Graeme didn't look like he was going to do it, but Jack got the best out of him after I'd retired. In many respects he was very similar to Bill Harris apart from the fact that he was a very good tough tackler. I think if Bill and Graeme had been able to play in the same team they would have complemented each other very well."
Gordon Jones.

JUNINHO

" Give him the ball and let him do the rest "

Born: Sao Paulo 22-02-73

Just as David Armstrong was Jack Charlton's 'little gem' during the 1970's, so Juninho is Bryan Robson's little gem two decades later. Hugely popular with Boro fans, the diminutive Brazilian's tricky skills have arguably made him the most exciting player ever to pull on the famous red and white shirt.

Juninho caused a sensation when he chose to join Boro ahead of a host of top European clubs in October 1995. Although the £4.75 million fee was more than Boro were looking to pay, it now looks a snip for a player who has frequently set alight the Premiership. It was hardly surprising that his former club Sao Paulo were initially reluctant to sell their prized asset but the persuasive powers of Bryan Robson convinced Juninho that Teesside was the place to be.

Juninho - real name Oswaldo Giroldo Junior - was rejected as 'too small' by his first club, Juventus of Brazil, and became an amateur with Corinthians before hitting the big time. He moved on to Ituano where his performances caught the attention of top Brazilian side Sao Paulo. With Juninho in a starring role, Sao Paulo won the World Club Championship in 1994, having already won the Super Copa in 1993 and the Recopa in both 1993 and 1994. Although Brazilians do not carefully record players' career records, it is believed he scored 15 goals in 101 games for Sao Paulo.

Named the Brazilian Footballer of the Year in 1995, he came to the attention of Boro boss Bryan Robson with an astonishing goal for his country against England at Wembley. Despite a last-gasp bid by Arsenal, Boro eventually got their man and Juninho made his debut in a 1-1 draw against Leeds United in November 1995 after 5,000 supporters had turned out to greet him on the day he arrived at the Cellnet Riverside Stadium. Although he struggled to maintain his best form, it was clear to see that Juninho's skills were a rarity in the modern game and he quickly fitted into his role just behind the main striker. In his second season with the club, he began to display his fabulous skills on a consistent basis to strike fear into opposing defenders and inspired Boro to the Coca-Cola Cup Final in April 1997.

Juninho's move from Brazil to Teesside was a nail-biting experience for the young star but he soon put the fear into British opponents.

BORO RECORD 1995/-

Season	Div	League App	League Gls	Cup App	Cup Gls	Total App	Total Gls
1995/96	P	20(1)	2	5	0	25(1)	2
1996/97	P	28	10	9	3	37	13
*Total		48(1)	12	14	3	62(1)	15

*Figures correct to 9.4.97

The Brazilian maestro salutes another piece of magic after clinching victory at Goodison in October 1996.

"His individual ability makes him an outstanding player. He's great to play alongside and sometimes you can't believe some of the things he does with the ball."
Curtis Fleming.

"Juninho has tremendous skill. He is the sort of player people want to see because he runs at people. He's a great player because he sees things two or three seconds before others. Unfortunately, sometimes his team-mates are not as quick-thinking as him."
Gordon Jones.

MY TOP 5
Juninho

1. Emerson
2. Bryan Robson
3. Fabrizio Ravanelli
4. Robbie Mustoe
5. Steve Vickers

"Juninho excites the fans and has the ability to make things happen on the pitch. That's why I brought him to England - he's a class player. We always knew he had the ability but he's settled in very well both in terms of the style of football and the way of life."
Bryan Robson.

"I've played with all the Brazilians who have come to England including Mirandinha at Newcastle but Juninho is the first to succeed. You just give him the ball and let him do the rest. On his day, there's nobody like him."
John Hendrie.

"Nobody has seen the likes of Juninho before at Middlesbrough. He is a terrific ball player with vision, great dribbling ability and he has got a heart as big as a lion."
Willie Maddren.

"I've seen him play for Brazil and for Middlesbrough. He has an outstanding fitness level, is a good passer, has good awareness and is very intelligent. And as well as being an individual, he is also a team player. He would fit into any side, given the right role."
Bruce Rioch.

"As a provider and maker of chances he is so quick. I didn't see Wilf Mannion play but I believe they would have similar balance. People say that Wilf used to glide over heavy pitches and that's what Juninho does. Skill always overcomes and Juninho also has a great work-rate with a massive will to win. He stands out because he wants to do well and, of course, he's a Brazilian international. His first touch is perfect."
Frank Spraggon.

"What can I say? I just think he's a brilliant little player. I can't say any more than that."
Chris Morris.

"He is a world class player, so slight but he has adapted to the English game. For one so diminutive, he is a fantastic player."
Pat Cuff.

"There is quality in everything he does. He works hard, is a good passer of the ball and with the right supply can score goals. And as well as being a superstar, he is also a team player."
Peter Davenport.

MY TOP 5
Mike Angus

1. Juninho
2. John Hickton
3. Stuart Boam
4. Willie Maddren
5. Craig Johnston

MY TOP 5
Clayton Blackmore

1
Juninho
2
Gary Pallister
3
John Hendrie
4
Emerson
5
Fabrizio Ravanelli

"Juninho has broken the mould in the way he has been a success over here. He's got superb skills but that doesn't necessarily mean a player will be a success in moving from a country like Brazil to England. But he has done so well and is probably the best of the foreigners."
Ian Baird.

"In a hotter climate, I'm sure we'd see an even better Juninho but he's still the best player ever to play for Middlesbrough. You just never know what he's going to do next and I'm not sure he does sometimes! He's got fantastic pace which causes defenders so much trouble. He has this ability to get his toe there before his opponent and nick it past them."
Clayton Blackmore.

"I enjoy playing alongside players like Juninho who are always looking to pass the ball to you. He brings other people into the game and, just as importantly, he is a great guy off the pitch."
Mikkel Beck.

"His touch is the best I've ever come up against - and that's only in training. The things he does are even more outrageous and breathtaking than during games. In one practice match, he nutmegged me three times even though I'd promised myself he wouldn't do it after the first time! Certainly, there's no English players with the skill he's got."
Michael Barron.

His spell-binding ability to run with the ball has enthralled all who have seen Juninho in red and white.

"I would have to say that Juninho is the quickest thing I've ever seen. It's just a shame that his colleagues do not have the same speed of thought and movement. He is streets ahead. He was the first big foreigner to move to the club and he has settled in without any problems and remained very loyal."
Graham Hedley.

"Juninho's got to be by far the best player I've ever seen in a Middlesbrough shirt. He's got such fantastic skill and a stunning turn of speed. He's a very special player."
Phil Stamp.

Juninho's Boro team-mates appreciate his desire for the ball and commitment to the cause.

"An all-round player who's the best dribbler of the ball I've ever seen."
Craig Hignett.

"He is the best young player in the world at the moment, pure quality. He's not just an individual player, he's also a team member and has stuck by the Boro. He's shown his commitment on the pitch, not in the tabloids."
Jamie Pollock.

"When he first came to England I thought he would probably fall away when the going got tough but he has proved me wrong. He is small and lightweight but can open up a defence. His passing and dribbling is quite special."
Brian Laws.

"He has been much better in his second season with the club. Juninho is one of the best players I've ever seen running with the ball."
Malcolm Allison.

MY TOP 5
Craig Liddle

1. Juninho
2. Fabrizio Ravanelli
3. Emerson
4. Nick Barmby
5. Bernie Slaven

"He has everything. Undoubtedly, he's one of the best players in the world. It did surprise me when he joined Middlesbrough but you can't help but learn from a player like Juninho simply by training with him every day."
Mark Summerbell.

"He's very quick and clever, sometimes a little too clever because his team-mates are not always on the same wavelength as him."
Mark Burke.

"He would be my number one choice because of his sheer skill. He's so quick and his speed of thought is incredible. He is the best I've ever seen, simple as that."
Craig Liddle.

"A lot has been said about Juninho but it's important to remember that he came to England from Brazil as a relatively unknown quantity for many people. Of course, he'd already won the Brazilian player of the year award but he still had a mountain to climb. But he has settled better than anyone could have hoped and now produces his best form on a regular basis."
Viv Anderson.

Gary PALLISTER

" The nearest thing to a footballing centre-half "

Born: Ramsgate 30-06-65

The tall defender took the first step on the road that led from the Northern League to the England side when Willie Maddren recruited him in 1985. Pallister's first connection with Boro had come in the shape of a reserve team trial in Malcolm Allison's time in charge of the club. The Teesside lad failed to impress and continued in the Northern League with Billingham Town. But Boro coach Willie Maddren kept his eye on the youngster and a year later Pallister signed for Boro.

The youngster made his Boro debut in the first game of the 1985/86 season. Unfortunately for Pallister, Boro lost the game 3-0 to Wimbledon and he was left on the sidelines for three months, before returning to cement a regular place in the centre of defence after a short loan spell with Darlington.

Pallister was a virtual ever-present as the club rose from the Third Division to the First under Bruce Rioch. He performed the rare feat of being called up by England while still in the Second Division and, after initially being withdrawn to help Boro prepare for the play-offs, he made his England debut against Hungary in 1988.

But when Boro dropped out of the top flight at the end of the 1988/89 season, Boro's prize asset inevitably interested the top clubs and Pallister moved on. Manchester United shelled out £2.3 million to take him to Old Trafford. He helped the club to their first Championship since 1967 when they lifted the title in 1993. Pallister has also collected FA Cup, League Cup and European Cup Winners Cup medals since leaving Boro. And the England caps have swelled, though Pallister missed out on both the 1992 and 1996 European Championships through injury.

Gary Pallister, pictured before taking part in Bernie Slaven's benefit match in 1996, has plenty to smile about - he finished third in the all-time list.

BORO RECORD 1985-89

Season	Div	League App	League Gls	Cup App	Cup Gls	Total App	Total Gls
1985/86	2	28	0	2	0	30	0
1986/87	3	44	1	10	0	54	1
1987/88	2	44	3	14	1	58	4
1988/89	1	37	1	3	0	40	1
1989/90	2	3	0	0	0	3	0
Total		**156**	**5**	**29**	**1**	**185**	**6**

England: 20 caps (2 with Boro) 0 gls.

Pallister, in pre-season training before the start of the 1988/89 campaign, shows the style that was soon to make him the country's most expensive player.

"We used to call him Go-Go Gadget after the TV cartoon character because people used to think they were past him and out would come this telescopic leg and get the ball. When he first came he was like Bambi on ice but as time went on he went from strength to strength.

Bruce Rioch used to try and knock him down a peg or two, they had a few arguments, but it never knocked the stuffing out of him. He was very down to earth with no airs and graces. As Alex Ferguson discovered later on, he never got flustered."
Alan Kernaghan.

"He was a little bit different. He was learning his trade at the time and learnt a lot from Tony Mowbray and even then he had something special. He had the speed and the height. Pally was dominant in the air, quick, had a nice touch and could play."
Steve Pears.

"To me, Pally and Tony Adams are the best defenders in the country. I played against him when he was at Middlesbrough and it was obvious then he was going to be special. To his raw talent, he added strength and maturity at United."
Bryan Robson.

"The most complete player for a particular position I ever saw. At his height there was no better centre-half. He was - and still is - a good tackler, reads the game well, passes perfectly, brings the ball out of defence, he's good in the air - the list goes on. He was an exceptional player with Boro and got much better with Manchester United."
Gary Gill.

"Pally was at Old Trafford when I first joined Manchester United and he was a class player. But he wasn't always world class, he listened and learned. He was very raw when he left Middlesbrough for United but still already had all the makings of a very good centre-back and he matured into a very special player."
Viv Anderson.

MY TOP 5
Viv Anderson

1. Gary Pallister
2. Graeme Souness
3. Juninho
4. John Hendrie
5. Stephen Pears

MY TOP 5
Gary Pallister

1 Graeme Souness
2 Tony Mowbray
3 Willie Maddren
4 Bernie Slaven
5 Colin Cooper

"I wouldn't pick him for his training ability! He was very comfortable on the ball, good in the air and had a bit of pace as well. He put me in mind of a young Alan Hansen in those days and I'm not surprised he went on to what he has achieved."
Trevor Senior.

"He wasn't the finished article at Middlesbrough but you could see he would be a good player. He is the nearest thing to a footballing centre-half. There are a lot of pretenders to that crown but he is the nearest thing."
Peter Davenport.

"I've always found Gary Pallister very hard to play against. He's a very intelligent centre-half who doesn't fall for strikers' tricks. He knows what his own strengths are and he uses them to his own advantage. He has been one of the best defenders in England over the last 10 years."
Jan Fjortoft.

"I used to watch Pally from the Holgate at Ayresome Park when I was a young lad and he was quality. Even then he was quick, good in the air and a strong tackler but he has become probably the best centre-back in England."
Phil Stamp.

"Coming from the non-league was a big step up but he was always comfortable on the ball for such a big lad. He learned a lot from playing alongside Tony Mowbray while Toddy and Bruce were able to bring the best out of him to give him the self-belief to go on and become a top player."
Dean Glover.

"He always looked tired but not too many could outstrip him."
Trevor Putney.

"Gary was so consistent while we had our successful period under Bruce Rioch at a time when the club really needed it. He has gone on to prove what a good player he is at Manchester United."
Tony Mowbray.

"I might be biased because he plays in my position but I would say he's the best in Britain, if not Europe. His positional sense is fantastic, he's very good in the air and three League championships - you can't argue with that record."
Phil Whelan.

"For Alex Ferguson to pay £2.3 million, when it was real money, to take him to Old Trafford shows just how much he was rated. He has gone on to become a top international performer and although he hadn't reached his peak when he was at Boro the fact that he has progressed so well means he gets my vote."
Lennie Lawrence.

"Pally was a great player who always did his job so well. At his height, he was the best centre-back in the country. Admittedly, he wasn't at his very best during his early days with Middlesbrough but I know from experience that, even then, he was not easy to replace!"
Simon Coleman.

Boro's pride: When Pallister earned an international call-up in April 1988, he became the first Boro star to play for England since David Armstrong eight years earlier.

Gary Pallister

Style and tenacity: Pallister in the thick of it against Liverpool during the 1988/89 season. Looking on is Paul Kerr.

"Pally may be my best mate but this vote is purely down to his footballing ability. He's such a classy defender and even when he was at Boro I used to say he was a cut above the rest. Most central defenders are rugged, Pally is the complete opposite. He is cultured, capable of bringing the ball out of defence and passing it, while chipping in with the odd goal, though I must say it was just the odd goal. He's won the lot with United and that's why he gets my vote."
Bernie Slaven.

"Gary Pallister is the reason why Manchester United have done so well in recent years. For many years before he arrived they had a good team but had a tendency to get results against the good teams and let themselves down against the likes of Wimbledon, who would outfight us in the air. Then Pally came and things changed, while he learned a lot playing alongside Steve Bruce. But even when he was at Middlesbrough and still relatively raw, he was class. As soon as he joined United, you could see he had filled a huge hole."
Clayton Blackmore.

"The man is sheer class. He exudes confidence. I would have loved to have seen him play with Nigel Pearson because I think they would have made a fantastic partnership."
Chris Morris.

"An excellent centre-half and, at the time he was with Boro, one of the few who could pass the ball as well as defend. It was always obvious that he would go further in the game than any of us."
Paul Kerr.

"He had a great partnership with Tony Mowbray. They were exceptional together and Pally has gone on to even better things."
Stuart Ripley.

"I played against Pallister when he was a young lad at Middlesbrough and you could see even then that he had the ability to go on and become a great player. He just had that something extra over other central defenders. Of course, he went on to realise that potential at Manchester United but he established his reputation at Middlesbrough."
Ian Baird.

MY TOP 5
Gary Gill

1. Gary Pallister
2. Juninho
3. Tony Mowbray
4. Stephen Bell
5. Stephen Pears

Wilf MANNION

" He was unbelievable "

Born: South Bank 16-05-18

A Boro career that was to span almost two decades and spawn a legend started when Boro boss Wilf Gillow brought the slight inside-forward to the club in September 1936. Mannion had been playing for South Bank St Peter's in the Teesside League.

The 18-year-old made his Boro debut in January 1937 in a 2-2 draw against Portsmouth at Ayresome Park, but had to wait a further three months before he next pulled on a first team shirt. But when he was called upon in December 1937 after another lengthy spell on the sidelines, he netted in successive games and took hold of a regular slot as Boro challenged for honours at the top of the First Division.

Just as success seemed just around the corner, war intervened and Mannion lost six seasons of top flight football. He continued to play for Boro in the early years of the war while serving in the Auxiliary Fire Service before being called up and earned his first international recognition in 1941 when he played in an unofficial international between England and Scotland.

Once the league programme resumed for the 1946/47 season, Mannion was back in his rightful place in the Boro side. He earned his first official England cap against Scotland at Wembley in April 1947. Then went on to collect 26 caps including playing in the 1950 World Cup in Brazil. He also represented Great Britain in a famous 7-2 win over the Rest of Europe.

As the 1948/49 season got underway, Mannion was missing from the starting line-up after refusing to re-sign for the club. He planned to move to Oldham Athletic and set up business in the town but Boro's price tag of £25,000 was too high for the Lancashire club and Mannion eventually resumed his Boro career in time to help steer the club away from relegation.

After five more seasons of top flight football, Boro were relegated at the end of the 1953/54 season and Mannion decided to call it a day at the age of 36.

Just a few months later, however, he was tempted back into football by Boro's Second Division rivals Hull City. Boro had retained Mannion's registration despite his retirement and Hull paid £5,000 for his services.

But Mannion only served Hull for one season. The Football League was unhappy when he refused to elaborate on newspaper articles he had written in his spell out of the game and he was suspended from playing in June 1955.

Mannion opted to play outside the league and turned out for Poole Town, King's Lynn, Haverhill Rovers and Earlstown before finally drawing the curtain on his illustrious career, aged 44, in 1962.

He returned to Teesside where he continues to live and is a regular visitor to the Cellnet Riverside Stadium.

Still at Boro after all those years: Mannion on an emotional lap of honour before the last ever league match at Ayresome Park.

BORO RECORD 1936-54

Season	Div	League App	Gls	Cup App	Gls	Total App	Gls
1936/37	1	2	0	0	0	2	0
1937/38	1	22	4	3	1	25	5
1938/39	1	38	14	4	1	42	14
1946/47	1	37	18	7	5	44	23
1947/48	1	35	1	3	1	38	2
1948/49	1	17	4	0	0	17	4
1949/50	1	38	6	3	1	41	7
1950/51	1	35	14	1	0	36	14
1951/52	1	39	11	3	2	42	13
1952/53	1	41	18	1	0	42	18
1953/54	1	37	9	2	1	39	10
Total		**341**	**99**	**27**	**11**	**368**	**110**

England: 26 caps (all with Boro) 11 gls.

Legends meet: Mannion chats with former England team-mate Sir Stanley Matthews at a sportmen's dinner in 1995.

"He was a classic footballer. Wilf could practically make the ball talk. Once he got control of the ball you had a hell of a job getting it back."
Micky Fenton.

"As a boy I was a huge Manchester United supporter but Wilf Mannion was the first player from another club who I really admired. He was the golden boy and I saw him play quite a few times at Old Trafford. He was brilliant. And when I later went to Middlesbrough and met him, it was a great moment for me."
Nobby Stiles.

"When I was a young person, I saw Wilf Mannion play and he made such a big impression on me that he was my first favourite player. His small frame belied all the talent and ability that was within him. He had total class. He was an entertainer with tremendous skill and technique and was a team player as well as an individual.

It was a pleasure to meet him in later life when I was manager of Middlesbrough. Whilst I was at the club I was in my office when Keith Lamb called me to say there were two people he would like me to meet. One was Wilf Mannion and the other George Hardwick. I walked in with two contracts and said: "Fill them in and put your own figures on them! I would have loved to have had them in my side."
Bruce Rioch.

"Everybody knows Wilf and I played for England together. In fact it seemed he scored more for England than he did for Middlesbrough. I remember one year in particular when Wilf scored eight goals for England yet only a handful all season for Boro. Still, Wilf was a very good player who played a very important role in a Boro side that used to attract massive crowds wherever they played."
George Hardwick.

MY TOP 5
Wilf Mannion

1. Micky Fenton
2. Ralph Milne
3. Bob Baxter
4. Bennie Yorston
5. Duncan McKenzie

"To me, Wilf was the best controller of the ball I've ever seen. I used to throw the ball out to him and he was facing me, then he would turn away and jump over the defender who was challenging him. He had a great positional sense and was very good tactically. He wasn't in the game for long, but for the short while he was involved he was fantastic."
Rolando Ugolini.

"Wilf had everything. He had the body swerve, was two-footed, could head the ball and could read the game from A to Z, It was a pleasure to play alongside him."
Harry Bell.

"When I first came into the Boro side during the early 1950s, Wilf was the only player who took time to think about the tactics of the game. Before my debut, he came over and told me: 'You know your strong points, you're a ball winner. Win it, look for me and I'll take it forward.' That was just what I needed. Then, soon after the war when I was a PT instructor in the RAF, based near Wolverhampton, we played Wolves - who were great at the time - and I expected us to get a right stuffing. But Wilf told me that one of their star players, Jimmy Mullen, was chicken-hearted and that I should whack him early on and I'd not have any trouble from him. He was right. We won the game and Wilf gave Billy Wright the run around."
Derek Stonehouse.

Wilf Mannion, in action during his hey-day, was Boro's all-time great for many who saw him play.

"He was my first idol as a kid. I used to go an watch the Boro with Wilf playing and he had everything. Everybody idolised him at the time and he starred at a time when there was a lot of great players about. He was even better because of that."
Alan Peacock.

"You can keep your George Bests, Wilf Mannion was far better and certainly one of the greatest players I've ever seen. The way he could sell defenders a dummy was like nothing you see nowadays. He wasn't particularly tall but he could outjump six foot defenders easily. Wilf Mannion was unbelievable."
Arthur Fitzsimons.

"Wilf had a silken touch.
He was physically slight
but he had a heart
as big as a football
and he never shirked anything.
He was unique."

Brian Clough.

Three opponents surround Wilf, the Golden Boy, as he attempts more football wizardry

MY TOP 5
Bruce Rioch

1
Wilf Mannion
2
Brian Clough
3
Graeme Souness
4
Fabrizio Ravanelli
5
Juninho

"Wilf was my idol as a boy. He had everything - even his heading ability was amazing and yet he was very small. Quite simply, he was head and shoulders above anyone else for club and country, he just shone out."
Mick McNeil.

MY TOP 5
Rolando Ugolini

1
Wilf Mannion
2
George Hardwick
3
Lindy Delapenha
4
Brian Clough
5
Dicky Robinson

"I always thought of him as like a ballerina on stage, his balance was amazing. He was a two-footed player and even though he was a small fella he could jump as high as a gazelle."
Ray Bilcliff.

Wilf was top with natural ability, he had a gift. I used to watch him when I was a schoolboy when he was everyones idol."
Billy Day.

"In his prime he was probably the best most people would have seen at Middlesbrough. When I was a young lad and first came to the club I sat in the corner for weeks wondering what I was doing at a club with players of his ability."
Geoff Walker.

Willie MADDREN

" The best uncapped defender of his era"

Born: Billingham 11-01-51

Maddren signed professional for Middlesbrough in June 1968. The youngster had been due to go to Leeds for a trial prior to joining Boro but broke his ankle playing for Port Clarence Juniors. He made his full Boro debut in a 3-2 defeat against Bury at the tail end of the 1968/69 season. He was employed as a forward by manager Stan Anderson and had an eventful first start, scoring a goal and breaking his nose.

In the following seasons, Maddren was used as a utility man through the team before settling in at centre-back where he established himself as one of the best defenders around, enjoying a telepathic-like partnership with Stuart Boam at the heart of the Boro defence. He won five England under-23 caps but never graduated to the full national side.

Maddren's career was ended by a serious knee injury and he played his last game away at West Brom in September 1978, aged just 26. He joined Hartlepool as coach but returned to Boro in 1983 and, on Jack Charlton's arrival - back at Boro after the sacking of Malcolm Allison - Maddren was promoted to first team coach. He was then made manager for the 1984/85 season on Charlton's recommendation.

In a time of turmoil and mounting debts, Maddren faced an uphill struggle to turn the club's fortunes around. In February 1986, he was sacked and replaced by Bruce Rioch.

After leaving the club, Maddren returned to running sports shops in the area. A crowd of 20,000 attended the Cellnet Riverside Stadium in August 1996 to see Boro play Inter Milan in a benefit match for Maddren as he battled against Motor Neurone Disease.

Twenty years after his last game for Boro, Willie Maddren is still fondly remembered by all who saw him play.

BORO RECORD 1968-78

Season	Div	League App	League Gls	Cup App	Cup Gls	Total App	Total Gls
1968/69	2	1(1)	1	0	0	1(1)	1
1969/70	2	10	0	1	0	11	0
1970/71	2	34	2	2	0	36	2
1971/72	2	40(2)	7	8	0	48(2)	7
1972/73	2	40	2	5	0	45	2
1973/74	2	42	3	5	0	47	3
1974/75	1	42	2	13	1	55	3
1975/76	1	41	2	15	1	56	3
1976/77	1	39	0	8	0	47	0
1977/78	1	4	0	1	0	5	0
Total		**293(3)**	**19**	**58**	**2**	**351(3)**	**21**

Maddren in action during Boro's 2-0 win at Coventry City on the final day of the 1974/75 season. He was ever-present throughout the campaign.

"He played alongside me in the centre of defence and we had a very good understanding. He was one of the only players that I never had to fall out with and shout at on the pitch because we gelled well together and knew each other's game. I was the physical bloke and Willie picked the bits up because he could play."
Stuart Boam.

"He started out as a striker when I was first at the club but Jack Charlton moved him back to centre-half. He read the game, was tremendous in the air and was also a smashing bloke to play with."
John Craggs.

"He was Mr Consistency. Willie read the game well and was a terrific back four player. He would have played more but for injuries."
Jim Platt.

"One of the best uncapped players in the country. Barring injuries, he would have played for England quite a few times. The injury he had to his knee didn't allow him to progress to that level. For a centre-half he had everything - he read the game well, was a good tackler and could pass the ball. He was also a good pro who would just get on with his job."
Ian Bailey.

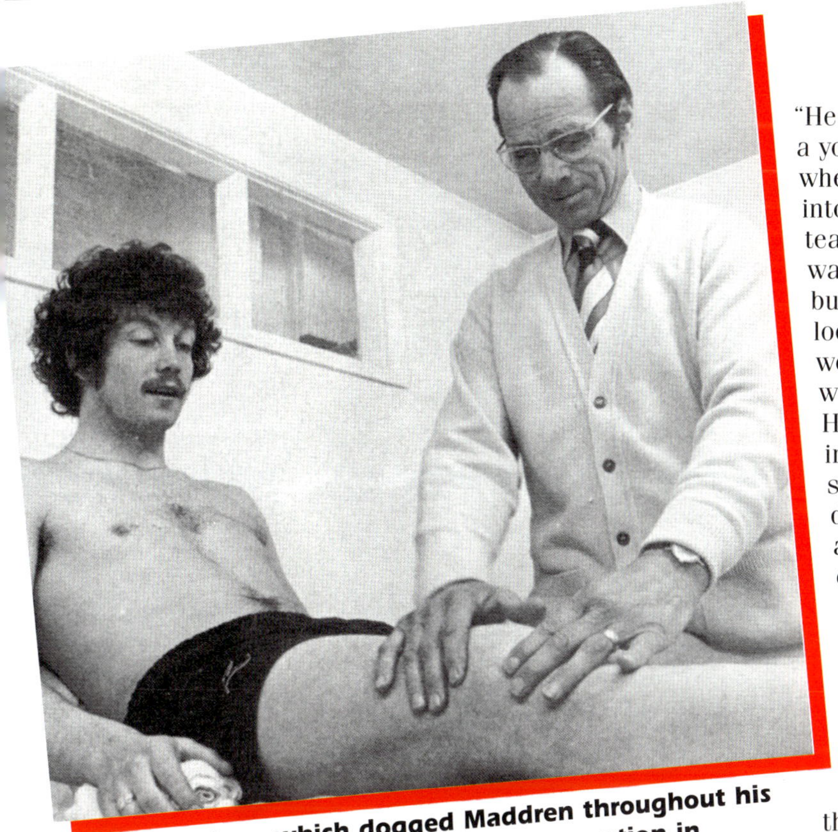

A knee problem, which dogged Maddren throughout his career, eventually ended it despite an operation in September 1977. Here club physiotherapist Lew Clayton examines the knee which was to bring his career to a premature end.

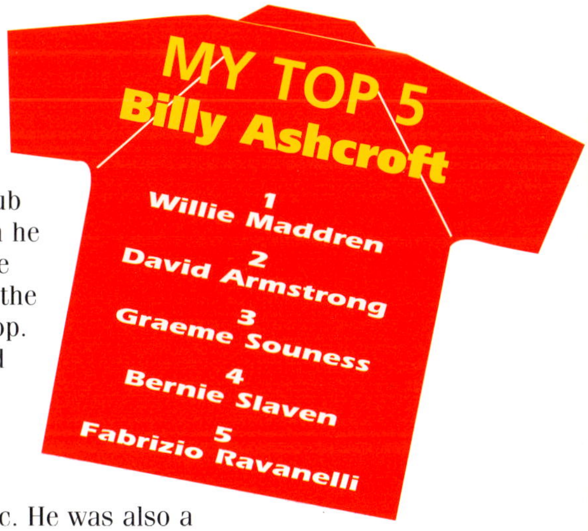

"He was only a young lad when he got into the team while I was at the club but even then he looked like he would go all the way to the top. He was good in the air, strong, determined and enthusiastic. He was also a sensible lad and listened to advice which a lot of youngsters tended to brush aside.

He was the sort of player who could play anywhere - centre back, midfield or even up front - and looked the part wherever he played. He had the potential to play for England and I think the fact that he was seen as a utility player may have counted against him. He was also so unfortunate to have a bad injury that cut short his career."
Hugh McIlmoyle.

"I never played with him, only against him, and he was a class centre-back. As a centre-forward I always preferred to play against physical defenders rather than skilful ones and Willie was definitely a skilful one. He was a very difficult opponent."
Mick Burns.

"Willie is the most consistent player I've seen and that's despite his injury problems. He was a bit like Paul McGrath in the way he rarely trained during the week yet he always gave 100% when he was on the park. Willie was never flustered."
Billy Ashcroft.

"In the team I played in Willie was vital. He was technically very good, had a great understanding of the game and had a great attitude. He was always first onto the training ground and the last one off it."
Graeme Souness.

"He was probably the best uncapped centre-back of the era. It was a tragedy that because of his knee injury he never played for England because he had pace, he was a good passer, strong and had a tremendous attitude. He also really looked after me when I was a young kid at the club."
Tony McAndrew.

"He formed a great partnership with Stuart Boam. The way they worked together was a pleasure to watch, they complemented each other. Willie read the game so well and was an all-round player. He could push up to centre-forward and create havoc there as well as playing at the back."
David Armstrong.

"He played on one leg most of the time and never trained - a bit like Paul McGrath today. But he was as good as McGrath and he was a pleasure to play alongside."
Terry Cooper.

"He was the best uncapped defender around at that time. He was an accomplished defender and unfortunate that he wasn't at a more successful or fashionable club because he would have been capped. At that time there was Colin Todd, Norman Hunter, Emlyn Hughes and Kevin Beattie who were all England internationals so there was an abundance of top defenders. But Willie had the ability to be compared with them."
David Mills.

Willie Maddren

"Willie was the same as John Hickton in that he could play anywhere. He played in midfield, at centre back and as a forward where I really fancied him. However, I simply could not afford to push him up because we needed him at the back. Apart from his injuries Willie was a rock solid player and perhaps being a one club man hindered his career. Maddren and Boam were the perfect combination at the back under Jack Charlton because they had started to mature by that point. With Graeme Souness in front of them they were very strong and it was no surprise Boro's goals against record was so good when they won the Second Division."
Stan Anderson.

"Willie was such a good player for such a long time and I'm sure he'll be the choice of many. He was an excellent reader of the game, he read it so well that he often knew what people were going to do before they made their move. He also had pace, was tremendous in the air for someone of his size and he had two good feet."
Irving Nattrass.

Although he feels he failed to fulfil his potential as a player, Maddren rarely missed a game for Boro over seven seasons from 1970 onwards.

MY TOP 5
John Mahoney

1. Willie Maddren
2. Graeme Souness
3. David Armstrong
4. David Mills
5. John Hickton

"He was my youth team coach when I started at the club and I will always owe him because he gave me my chance in football. He gave me my debut when he was manager. He is one of the few people in football who I owe a debt to, He was also a player of extreme ability. His career was cut short when he could have gone on to play for England."
Colin Cooper.

"He gave me my first chance in football. He was in charge of the youth team and then became manager. His door was always open. As a player he had a fantastic left foot and phenomenal distribution."
Peter Beagrie.

"If it hadn't been for Kevin Beattie, Willie would probably have played for England. He was a classy central defender who wasn't a sweeper or centre-half, more of a partner of a centre-half. He used to tidy up at the back and he was strong in the air for a man who wasn't massive. A class player."
Kelham O'Hanlon.

MY TOP 5
Irving Nattrass

1. Willie Maddren
2. Graeme Souness
3. David Armstrong
4. David Hodgson
5. Mark Proctor

Brian CLOUGH

" His goalscoring record is unsurpassed "

Born: Middlesbrough 21-03-35

One of the most prolific goalscorers in post-war English football. Clough initially began his working life as a clerk with industrial giants ICI and playing regional football with local sides Billingham Synthonia and Great Broughton.

Eventually, and without surprise, Clough joined Boro as an amateur in 1951 and worked his way up to a first team debut against Barnsley in 1955.

An exceptionally brave and confident player, he scored his first goal against Leicester City a few weeks after his debut. Although his appearances were restricted during the season of his debut he became the first choice on manager Bob Dennison's team-sheet when the 1956/57 season commenced.

Throughout his time with Boro, Clough had an incredible scoring ratio of almost one goal per game played, with 204 goals in 222 games. Sadly, despite this, Boro could not hoist themselves to a promotion position in Division Two and the prolific striker was often at odds with the club.

Throughout his time he often submitted transfer requests and in 1959 nine of his teammates signed a petition asking for the captaincy to be taken away from him.

His international career was restricted to just two full caps and three under-23 appearances for England, which was nothing short of criminal considering his record.

A transfer request was eventually accepted in July 1961 and Clough moved to local rivals Sunderland for £45,000, who themselves were now a Second Division side. The goals continued to come at Roker Park, but with 53 already under his belt he suffered a serious knee injury against Bury on Boxing Day 1962 which ended his career.

Clough soon joined the Roker Park coaching staff before embarking on one of the most successful managerial careers in the modern game. After steadying a desperate ship at Hartlepool, Clough, together with former Boro keeper Peter Taylor as his second in command, steered Second Division Derby County to promotion, then the First Division title in 1972. He repeated the feat in 1978 with Nottingham Forest and bettered his European Cup semi-final with Derby, by winning the competition twice in 78 and 79.

Further trophies followed at the City Ground throughout the 1980's before he finally retired from the club following relegation in 1993. The major disappointment in Clough's managerial career mirrored that of his playing days - lack of recognition by his country. Along with being virtually ignored as a player, he was passed over for the England manager's position on several occasions.

Almost a goal a game. A record to smile about.

BORO RECORD 1955-61

Season	Div	League App	Gls	Cup App	Gls	Total App	Gls
1955-56	2	9	3	0	0	9	3
1956-57	2	41	38	3	2	44	40
1957-58	2	40	40	2	2	42	42
1958-59	2	42	43	1	0	43	43
1959-60	2	41	39	1	1	42	40
1960-61	2	40	34	2	2	42	36
Total		**213**	**197**	**9**	**7**	**222**	**204**

England: 2 caps (both with Boro) 0 gls.

Brian Clough

A big thumbs-up from the one and only Cloughie in front of the Holgate before watching Boro play Reading in February 1995. It was the first time he had seen a full game of any sort since retiring as manager of Nottingham Forest the previous May.

"His goalscoring record is unsurpassed. It's a record that is second to none. I saw him play in his early days and again in later life and his anticipation in the box was superb, his reading of the game was excellent and he had the awareness of play. Those were all great qualities for a goalscorer."
Bruce Rioch.

"I played for Brian at Forest but Old Big Head never talked about his playing days too much! But I have seen him on videos and his goalscoring record speaks for itself."
Peter Davenport.

"The amount of goals he scored per game was phenomenal. I played against him when he was a teenager and he was extremely confident in front of goal and good in the air. He was a player who wanted service from his midfield and was always shouting "give me the ball, give me the ball". It surprised me he didn't win more caps for England."
Malcolm Allison.

"With Brian it was simply his goalscoring. In our forward line he was the king pin, everything went through him and he delivered the goods."
Alan Peacock.

"Brian did what everybody wanted to do - score goals - week in week out. He put the ball in the net more often and consistently than any other Middlesbrough player I've ever seen.
"I played with him once in Gordon Jones testimonial game and although he didn't score, he headed one ball which showed very clearly what a tremendous scorer he was."
John O'Rourke.

"Like Cloughie I was a centre forward and I appreciated his obvious ability. His goalscoring record was second to none. I remember being brought down to Middlesbrough by a scout when I was a kid to see Boro play Leyton Orient, Cloughie was a natural, he just had the knack of scoring goals."
Arthur Horsfield.

MY TOP 5
Brian Clough

1. Wilf Mannion
2. George Hardwick
3. Micky Fenton
4. Alan Peacock
5. Rolando Ugolini

"Brian was ice cold - he didn't know fear when the ball was coming into the box. He had the ability to turn bad passes and crosses into good ones."
Billy Day.

"His goalscoring record is second to none, It stands comparison with anybody in the game and you would have to be quite a player to score the sheer amount of goals that he did."
Gary Walsh.

Cloughie captured in typical goal scoring action.

MY TOP 5
Arthur Horsfield

1. Brian Clough
2. Alan Peacock
3. Cyril Knowles
4. Mick McNeil
5. Ian Gibson

"My dad used to take me on the cross bar of his bike to see Cloughie play when I was about six years old. We used to go in the bob end and Cloughie was my hero I used to love watching him from my position on the wall."
Geoff Butler.

"Cloughie could score goals from anywhere but he also worked hard. I liked the way he played football. Unlike many seem to think, he wasn't a greedy player and would often play the ball out wide to bring the wingers into the game. I was fortunate enough to play alongside him when he left Middlesbrough for Sunderland and it was obvious he was a fantastic finisher. I actually think he was even better at Sunderland than he was at Middlesbrough."
Dicky Rooks.

"He gets my vote for his goalscoring ability. He had the best shot ever, he was brilliant, I've never seen anybody like him. You can't compare the forwards now because the ball is so much lighter."
Ray Yeoman.

"The best goalscorer Middlesbrough ever had. He was arrogant but he had to be and people say he didn't work a lot but he just kept scoring goals and that was what counted."
John Craggs.

"He was always a domineering character but I still felt the round robin by the players to take away his captaincy was very sneaky. I was one of the few who didn't sign it because I was a friend of his, like Peter Taylor. He was loud-mouthed but his work in the opposition penalty box was fantastic. Initially, he only ever looked for goals and refused to lay the ball off to team-mates but he improved as time went on."

Derek Stonehouse.

MY TOP 5
Malcolm Allison

1. Brian Clough
2. Emerson
3. Craig Johnston
4. Fabrizio Ravanelli
5. Juninho

Brian Clough is pictured (front row, centre) with the Boro first team squad before the start of the 1955/56 season. Other members of Boro's Best pictured include Rolando Ugolini (back row, fourth left) Bill Harris (back row, second right) and Micky Fenton (middle row, second left)

After an amazing 6-6 draw at Charlton in 1960, hat-trick hero Brian Clough asked his team-mates pointedly, "If we score seven goals next week, do you think we'll get two points?"

Tony MOWBRAY

" A born leader and Boro through and through "

Born: Saltburn 22-11-63

Captain Courageous, Mr Middlesbrough, or simply Mogga, Tony Mowbray was the linchpin around which the Boro team was built for more than a decade. A rock at centre-half and one of the most respected captains in the club's history, Mowbray stood firm in the Boro defence through the turbulent liquidation times and was a key figure in the resurgence under Bruce Rioch.

Mowbray joined the club he had supported as a boy when he was signed up on schoolboy forms in 1978. He had stood on the Holgate End as a youngster and progressed through the ranks to make his Boro debut against Newcastle in September 1982, when he marked Kevin Keegan.

He was a regular throughout the mid-80s and was an inspirational captain for five years after the liquidation saga of 1986. It was Bruce Rioch who famously commented: "If you were in a rocket ship going to the moon, the man you would want sitting next to you would be Tony Mowbray". Mogga, as he was known to his team-mates, was part of the team that climbed into the First Division in 1988 and, at the end of the 1988/89 season, he was also called up along with defensive partner Gary Pallister for an England B tour.Despite being injured, Mowbray had the honour of leading Boro out in the Zenith Data Systems Cup final at Wembley in March 1990.

But the stint in the top flight was short-lived and after another two years in the Second Division, Mowbray decided it was time to move and made a £1 million switch to Celtic, although he returned soon afterwards for a much deserved testimonial match. Injuries began to play a part as Mowbray spent periods out of the team at Parkhead and he eventually moved to Ipswich in October 1995 for £300,000. Unfortunately, the injury problems have continued since the move to East Anglia.

Tony Mowbray is remembered as one of Boro's all-time greatest captains.

BORO RECORD 1982-91

Season	Div	League App	League Gls	Cup App	Cup Gls	Total App	Total Gls
1982/83	2	25(1)	0	5	0	30(1)	0
1983/84	2	33(2)	1	3(1)	0	36(3)	1
1984/85	2	40	3	4	0	44	3
1985/86	2	35	4	3	0	38	4
1986/87	3	46	7	12	0	58	7
1987/88	2	44	3	14	2	58	5
1988/89	1	37	3	7	0	44	3
1989/90	2	28	2	10	0	38	2
1990/91	2	40	3	12(1)	1	52(1)	4
1991/92	2	17	0	3	0	20	0
Total		**346(3)**	**26**	**73(2)**	**3**	**419(5)**	**29**

Tony Mowbray led out the first Boro team to play at Wembley in the ZDS Cup final 1990, despite missing the game with a pelvic injury. Mogga was given the role by manager Colin Todd as a reward for his sterling service for the club.

What do you think of this team, Bernie? Mowbray discusses team tactics with Bernie Slaven before Slaven's benefit match. Mowbray, unable to play due to injury, was manager of the Boro All-Star team.

"Tony was a young lad in the reserves when I first played with him. He never looked much like a footballer but he had a heart the size of a bin lid and matured well at Middlesbrough in a similar way to Tony McAndrew. You always need people like Tony Mowbray in your side."
Terry Cochrane.

"Mogga was such a great help to Pally while they played together at Boro, he was an excellent foil for him. Mogga was completely different to Pally in the respect that he was the sort who would put his head in where it hurts. Mogga was a leader by example, a player with great self-discipline."
Bernie Slaven.

"For me being a goalkeeper, the ones right in front of you are the most important. You never had to say too much to Tony, he would just get on with it and was very reliable."
Steve Pears.

"He was a great player to have alongside you in the centre of defence and his leadership was second to none."
Gary Pallister.

"For the time I was there, he was our leader. He was a good player who got himself England B caps and was unlucky not to have progressed with Gary Pallister. He was Mr Middlesbrough, Boro through and through."
Colin Cooper.

MY TOP 5
Tony Mowbray

1. Graeme Souness
2. Gary Pallister
3. Stephen Pears
4. Bernie Slaven
5. John Hickton

"I was always very impressed with Tony before I joined the club because he seemed to be the main man at the back for Middlesbrough. When I played alongside him, I realised just how good he was and appreciated his value to the club. He was a born leader and was always prepared to put his head in dangerous places and get it kicked for the cause. He was, in effect, Mr Boro."
Robbie Mustoe.

Mowbray in action during a pre-season friendly before the start of the 1989/90 campaign.

Tony Mowbray

Thanks for the memories: Supporters cheer Mowbray during a lap of honour before the last league game at Ayresome Park.

"Mogga was the local lad who myself and all the other young players looked up to at Ayresome Park - even though he wasn't much older than us. He set the standards and he was the player I wanted to emulate. Unlike some players there was nothing 'big time' about Mogga, he always had time for a word of encouragement. He wasn't blessed with outstanding ability but he was so committed and whole-hearted that he had an aura about him that lifted players around him. He was the perfect Middlesbrough captain. Perhaps the biggest compliment I can pay him is that Gary Pallister wouldn't have looked half the player he was without Mogga alongside him."
Lee Turnbull.

I've spoken to a lot of football people who didn't really rate Tony like I did but perhaps you had to play with him to know just how good he was. Even though he wasn't blessed with the best ability, he was certainly the best centre-half I played alongside. He enjoyed playing so much and always worked so hard."
Ian Baird.

"Defensively he was solid but his best quality was his leadership. I didn't pick him because of his popularity but everybody liked and respected him and that made him a particularly good captain."
Alan Foggon.

"He was a leader, he had something about him. He was only two years older than me but it felt like 20."
Ian Ironside.

"He formed a great partnership with Gary Pallister. Mogga was the more dominant of the two and an exceptionally good captain. The fans appreciated that he was Middlesbrough through and through."
Stuart Ripley.

"Tony was so helpful to me when I first moved to Middlesbrough, he was that kind of guy. On and off the field, he was Middlesbrough through and through. In fact, I was surprised he ever left Boro because I really thought he would be one of those club men who would go on to manage the team."
Simon Coleman.

"He was our very own Captain Marvel, a superb man to follow. He was totally professional in everything he did."
Jamie Pollock.

"Inspirational - that was Mogga. A man who led by example and never gave up. His Captain Courageous nickname was very appropriate."
Gary Gill.

"Mowbray was a great leader and a good player, respected by all of his team-mates, and the fans loved him. I doubt there's many players who received the same sort of affection from all the supporters as Mowbray."
Michael Barron.

MY TOP 5
Trevor Putney

1. Tony Mowbray
2. Fabrizio Ravanelli
3. Emerson
4. Gary Pallister
5. Stuart Ripley

Stephen PEARS

" One of the best keepers never to have played for England "

Born: Brandon 22-01-62

Boro's consistent number one saw his career lift off when he moved from Manchester United to Boro. Pears went from being understudy to the England keeper to the verge of national recognition in his own right after making the switch to Ayresome Park.

Pears joined United as a 14-year-old but chances were limited at Old Trafford by the presence of England keeper Gary Bailey at the head of the United pecking order. Pears' first link with Boro came in 1983 when Malcolm Allison took him to Teesside on loan. He made an inspirational debut in a 2-0 win over Cardiff and Boro were quoted £80,000 to make the move permanent. An appeal was launched but the target wasn't reached and Pears returned to Old Trafford.

Two years later, Willie Maddren had taken over the helm at Ayresome and Pears finally became a Boro player. Pears made the number one shirt his own as Boro climbed through the divisions under Bruce Rioch. Back in Division Two, Pears had to contest the slot with Kevin Poole but when Boro once again challenged for promotion in the 1991/92 season, he was back between the sticks. His form that year caught the eye of England boss Graham Taylor and he was called into the England squad. It proved to be a brief flirtation with the international scene as Pears was forced out of the squad with a fractured cheekbone, never to be picked again.

The arrival of Alan Miller pushed Pears out of the team for the start of the 1994/95 - his testimonial year - season and his last appearance was an inauspicious one - a 5-1 defeat against Luton. He was released at the end of the season and had 12 months with Liverpool before returning to the North-east to join Hartlepool.

Pears kept a remarkable 27 clean sheets during the 1986/87 league season.

BORO RECORD 1983-95

Season	Div	League App	Gls	Cup App	Gls	Total App	Gls
1983/84	2	12	0	2	0	14	0
1985/86	2	38	0	5	0	43	0
1986/87	3	46	0	12	0	58	0
1987/88	2	43	0	12	0	55	0
1988/89	1	26	0	7	0	33	0
1989/90	2	25	0	8	0	33	0
1990/91	2	27	0	10	0	37	0
1991/92	2	45	0	14	0	59	0
1992/93	P	26	0	3	0	29	0
1993/94	1	46	0	9	0	55	0
1994/95	1	5	0	3	0	8	0
Total		**339**	**0**	**85**	**0**	**424**	**0**

Pears pictured in the 1990/91 season when he helped the club reach the Second Division play-offs under Colin Todd's management.

"Between 1986 and 1990, Pears was one of the best keepers in the country. I'd never seen any player with an attitude like his, he hated getting beat and picking the ball out of the net. It was his drive which made him stand out from the rest."
Gary Hamilton.

"Pearsy may have been at the back end of his career when I came to Middlesbrough but he had done ever so well for the club for a full decade. He got to the verge of the England squad and rightly so because he was a very good goalkeeper at his peak."
Viv Anderson.

"He was a very good and reliable keeper. A tremendous shot-stopper who enjoyed himself tremendously in training and was always good fun to compete against."
Robbie Mustoe.

"He gained us promotion with a lot of match-winning performances. He was a great shot-stopper. Pearsy was a quiet man but very professional and a hard trainer."
Jimmy Phillips.

"He was such a nice guy on and off the field. He was a good shot-stopper, commanding in the box. He wasn't the biggest of keepers but he was good at organising at the back and made some good saves in important games."
Trevor Senior.

The £80,000 Boro paid for Stephen Pears in 1985 was over a third of manager Willie Maddren's total transfer budget of just £200,000. But Maddren still rated Pears as his best buy.

"He was another bargain buy by Willie Maddren and, in my opinion, he was the best goalkeeper to have played for Middlesbrough. He was a good pro with a great attitude. He was also involved at a time when the club was going through difficulties but he was still outstanding."
David Mills.

"As a keeper, Pearsy was almost complete. He used to dominate the box and tell defenders where to go, while he was a great shot-stopper. He was an extremely dedicated keeper who performed consistently well for 10 years. His red hair also gave him a shocking temper!"
Bernie Slaven.

"Pearsy's a nice fella and a fantastic keeper. He was a great shot-stopper at Boro with great reflexes."
Craig Hignett.

"I learnt a lot from Pearsy. I used to love watching him play and he was unlucky not be capped by England."
Ben Roberts.

"He won us many games that we had no right to win. Pearsy was a fantastic servant to the club and a great keeper."
Jamie Pollock.

"Pearsy proved himself over 10 years in three different divisions - he was a great goalkeeper. He was Mr Consistent and you always knew you could rely on him."
Simon Coleman.

Pears was ripe for picking by England during the early 1990s. Here he shows the safest pair of hands in Boro's history.

"Steve taught me everything I know about goalkeeping when I was at Old Trafford. We didn't have a goalkeeping coach but Steve was brilliant and I rate him very highly."
Gary Walsh.

"When I'm talking to our younger players at Ipswich I always try to encourage them to be like Pearsy. Whether it was a five-a-side or an important first team match, his attitude was always the same. He hated conceding goals. He was aggressive and dedicated."
Tony Mowbray.

"He's an absolutely outstanding keeper and a great guy. He really helped me settle in at the club, which must have been hard for him as I was there to take his place. I remember he had one sensational season around 1992 when he was called up for the England squad. He was a pleasure to work with."
Alan Miller.

"Pearsy's debut for Boro was one of the best performances I have ever witnessed. I think he got 10 out of 10 in the newspapers the following morning which tells a story in itself. He was a very fine, consistent goalkeeper who you could rely on. He was a great shot-stopper, confident and a loyal servant to the club."
Gary Gill.

MY TOP 5
Stephen Pears

1. Tony Mowbray
2. Gary Pallister
3. Colin Cooper
4. Bernie Slaven
5. Stuart Ripley

"He was probably the best goalkeeper I have played in front of. He was a nice fella but he had a wicked temper when pushed. You certainly knew about it if you got on the wrong side of him, he would chase you the length and breadth of the country!"
Alan Kernaghan.

Bernie SLAVEN

" One of the best goalscorers any club could have "

Born: Paisley 13-11-60

It was an unusual transfer saga that brought Slaven to Middlesbrough in October 1985. The Scot had been top scorer in his home country in the previous season, netting 31 times for Albion Rovers. But the former Morton, Airdrie and Queen of the South striker had refused to re-sign for his club in the close season and was working as a part-time gardener. He took the step of writing to every First and Second Division side in England asking for a trial. And it was Boro's Willie Maddren that responded and eventually picked Slaven up for a bargain £25,000. The deal brought to Teesside a player who was to rank among the club's best ever goalscorers.

Slaven made his Boro debut at Leeds before scoring in his first game at Ayresome Park the following week against Bradford City. Slaven's career spanned the liquidation saga and managers Maddren, Rioch, Todd and Lawrence. And as the team's fortunes fluctuated, Slaven continued to score regularly - he was top scorer for six consecutive seasons.

He also came to the attention of former Boro boss Jack Charlton and was picked for the Republic of Ireland, qualifying through his Irish grandfather. He made his debut against Wales in 1990 and scored Ireland's goal in a 1-1 draw. He was in Ireland's squad for the World Cup in Italy that year but was not used by Charlton.

Lennie Lawrence increased Slaven's use as a substitute through the 1991/92 season and when Boro rose into the Premier League in the following term, his appearances became more infrequent and before the season ended in relegation, Slaven had moved to Port Vale. After a further year at the Potteries club, he returned to the North-east to link up with Darlington before retiring with a persistent back injury in 1995.

Slaven in action at Loftus Road in September 1992.

BORO RECORD 1985-93

Season	Div	League App	Gls	Cup App	Gls	Total App	Gls
1985/86	2	32	8	2	1	35	9
1986/87	3	46	17	12	5	58	22
1987/88	2	44	21	14	3	58	24
1988/89	1	36(1)	15	3	1	39(1)	16
1989/90	2	46	21	13	11	59	32
1990/91	2	41(5)	16	11(1)	3	52(6)	19
1991/92	2	28(10)	16	9(2)	2	37(12)	18
1992/93	P	13(5)	4	1(2)	0	14(7)	4
Total		**286(21)**	**118**	**69(5)**	**28**	**355(26)**	**146**

Eire: 7 caps(all with Boro) 1 gl.

Slaven, holding his son Dominic, salutes the supporters before his benefit match at the Cellnet Riverside Stadium in 1996.

"In my time at Boro he was the best finisher I had ever seen. I used to get the brunt of it in training. He didn't strike the ball, he passed it into the net. If he had gone elsewhere I think he would have done as well as Pallister but, like me, he was happy to stay at the club."
Steve Pears.

"He was frustrating sometimes with his off-sides but his eye for goal was second to none and he was cool and calm in front of goal. He was always the player to be in the right place at the right time."
Dean Glover.

MY TOP 5
Alan Kernaghan

1
Bernie Slaven
2
Steve Pears
3
Tony Mowbray
4
Jim Platt
5
Gary Pallister

Three of Boro's Best: Slaven (centre) together with Curtis Fleming (left) and John Hendrie, shows his appreciation to the fans during an open-top bus ride through Middlesbrough town centre after the promotion success of 1992.

"He is probably the best finisher I have played with. I would say Alan Shearer is the all-round best centre-forward but Bernie was an incredible finisher."
Stuart Ripley.

"The man is a legend. When I was at Arsenal there was a lad there from Middlesbrough and he never shut up about this guy Bernie Slaven. When I joined Boro I realised how big he was in the town, whereas before I had only really known him for his goal celebration. He was a superb finisher."
Alan Miller.

"He was a class finisher. The price we paid for him must mean he's one of the best value for money signings ever. A fantastic player."
Curtis Fleming.

"Mr Slaven is the best goalscorer I've ever played with. He was completely dedicated, even in five-a-sides where he simply wanted to score goals. Bernie's goals were crucial to our success."
Tony Mowbray.

"For the five years we were together as a group at the club he was leading scorer every single season, especially in the promotion years, but even when we were relegated he still got goals. He was one of the main reasons we did so well."
Colin Cooper.

"How could I not vote for Bernie when he passed the ball to me so much during our days together? I am joking of course - even in his benefit game he didn't pass to me! Seriously though, Bernie's goals speak volumes. He was one of those players who was always likely to get a goal. Even in training, he was always the best finisher I've seen."
Ian Baird.

"Bernie is without doubt the best finisher I have ever seen in training. If the ball was on his left foot, it didn't matter from what angle or distance, he would stick it in the net."
Robbie Mustoe.

David ARMSTRONG

" He was Mr Consistent "

Born: Durham 26-12-54

Midfielder David Armstrong holds an incredible Boro record that is unlikely ever to be surpassed. Over a seven year period, Boro fans never failed to see Armstrong turning out for the club and his record for consecutive appearances stands as testimony to his consistency on the left side of Boro's midfield.

Boro scout George Wardle was responsible for bringing the young Armstrong to Middlesbrough aged just nine. Wardle then watched Armstrong progress from schoolboy to amateur to apprentice and to sign on as a professional on New Year's Eve 1971. The full graduation to the Boro first team swiftly followed when the 17-year-old ran out as a substitute against QPR in March 1972.

Within a year Armstrong had cemented a regular slot on the left side of Boro's midfield and after missing Boro's trip to Huddersfield in March 1973, he started the phenomenal run of 356 consecutive league and cup games for Boro. The next time Armstrong's name was to be missing from the Boro teamsheet was for the visit of Nottingham Forest in September 1980.

Armstrong's international honours initially came in the form of England under-23 and B caps but he was called up by Bobby Robson for a full cap against Australia in May 1980. Sadly, it was to be the only occasion Armstrong appeared in an England shirt while with Boro, though he won two more caps later.

In October 1980, Armstrong, at the age of just 25, was awarded a testimonial against Boro's 1973/74 promotion-winning team. Less than 12 months later, Armstrong, after more than 400 games for the club he left to join Southampton for a fee of £600,000.

He went on to play more than 200 games for the Saints before ending his career with Bournemouth. He still lives on the south coast today and is in charge of commercial operations for Waterlooville FC having previously worked for Hampshire schools as a sports liaison officer.

David Armstrong provided the crucial left-sided balance to Jack Charlton's promotion winning side.

BORO RECORD 1971-79

Season	Div	League App	Gls	Cup App	Gls	Total App	Gls
1971/72	2	5(1)	0	0	0	5(1)	0
1972/73	2	19(1)	1	1(1)	0	20(2)	1
1973/74	2	42	5	5	1	47	6
1974/75	1	42	5	14	3	56	8
1975/76	1	42	6	17	4	59	10
1976/77	1	42	8	9	4	51	12
1977/78	1	42	6	9	3	51	9
1978/79	1	42	11	4	0	46	11
1979/80	1	42	11	6	3	48	14
1980/81	1	39	6	6	0	45	6
Total		**357(2)**	**59**	**71(1)**	**18**	**428(3)**	**77**

England: 3 caps (1 with Boro) 0 gls.

David Armstrong

"He was very special. People never appreciated him as much as he deserved. He was the perfect left-sided midfield player. He worked the wing, could pass, score goals, he was a good header of the ball and if you were in trouble at the back you found him there as well. We had perfect balance with him in the side. He should have played more for England than he did but Bobby Robson played him out on the wing which was ridiculous."
John Neal.

"David was very consistent. He was great running forward and had a hell of a left foot on him. He played all those consecutive games and never got injured. It's funny that when he did get his first bad injury it ended his career."
Jack Charlton.

MY TOP 5
David Armstrong

1. John Hickton
2. Stuart Boam
3. Graeme Souness
4. Willie Maddren
5. Eric McMordie

"He had great vision for a guy so young. A lot of people thought he was older than he was because of his lack of hair. He could fall in and help at the back, get forward and support other people and create great crosses from the left side."
Bobby Murdoch.

No way through. David Armstong blocks the way to goal against Bristol City.

"I've seen him play a lot on club videos from the 1970s and he was a good player who scored lots of goals."
Emerson.

"Spike. We used to hang his kit up after every game for the next week because it never got dirty. He used to say: 'When you've got as much skill as me you don't need to tackle'. For somebody to play 300 odd consecutive games in the First Division, or Premier League as it is now, is incredible. He had a great left peg and gave the team balance on the left hand side. He was a very under-rated player outside Middlesbrough."
Kelham O'Hanlon.

"Best left-sided player I've ever seen and that's not just for Boro. We used to call him Einstein because he was a genius. He wasn't very consistent though - 300 odd games without injury - but he was half decent!"
Billy Ashcroft.

Armstrong prepares to give chase to Wolves' Willie Carr in a league game at Molineux during the 1980/81 season.

MY TOP 5
John Neal

1. David Armstrong
2. Tony McAndrew
3. Craig Johnston
4. Bosco Jankovic
5. David Hodgson

"Spike was the worst player to play against. He could score goals from nowhere in that he used to drift into positions and get on the end of things. He was superb in the air and he was Boro's top scorer for two seasons. A great left foot."
Irving Nattrass.

"People kept saying he never tackled and that's why he played so long but he was an excellent player."
Jim Platt.

"He played so many games and you're no chump doing that, especially under Jack Charlton. He didn't look particularly outstanding at any one thing but he did the job very well and made it look simple."
Pat Cuff.

"He was Mr Consistent. He never failed to turn in a good performance. He was steady and consistent and had the sweetest left foot, he could put the ball on a sixpence. He was one of the originators of the wing-back position and ran the whole left side."
Malcolm Smith.

"He was very consistent over a long period of time and always seemed to pose a threat to the opposition. He should have got more recognition. What stood out was his great left peg - and his bald head on the TV!"
Peter Davenport.

"Spike was a freak of his time when you consider the number of games he played when he was still a young lad. He had a marvellous engine - up and down the pitch - and a great left peg. He was also a character in his own way."
John Mahoney.

EMERSON

" Strong, but he's also got all the tricks "

Born: Rio de Janeiro 12-04-72

The new Bryan Robson. That was the tag Emerson Moises Costa carried with him when he joined Boro in a £4m move in May 1996. This superbly gifted midfielder may not look anything like his manager but there is no getting away from their similarities in style. Like Robbo, Emmo covers every inch of the pitch, tackles hard and scores goals. But it hasn't all been plain sailing for the Brazilian.

Emerson has had to do much of his settling in to a new way of life in the public glare. At the same time, he has had no such problems in adapting to the English style of football and was a revelation during his first two months on Teesside when many pundits tipped him for stardom. Stories about how he and his wife were struggling to settle down on Teesside adversely affected his form on the pitch but Emerson bounced back to his best alongside his compatriot, Juninho.

Although his talents are now unquestionable, Emerson's rise to the top was far from straight forward. He began his playing days with top Brazilian side Flamengo but found opportunities hard to come by and moved on to Curitiba. After taking advice, he switched to Portugal in 1991 in an attempt to make the big time and impressive displays for Belenenses over the following three years clinched a move to Porto. It was there, under the management of former England boss Bryan Robson, that he developed into a world class midfielder, helping Porto to win successive league titles. The winner of the 1996 Portuguese player of the year award, Emerson also starred in the European Champions League.

Much sought after, he was linked with Sampdoria, Fiorentina, Inter Milan and Roma but chose Boro when Bryan Robson laid down the gauntlet of helping Boro win a first major honour. His early displays at the Cellnet Riverside Stadium attracted unwanted interest from Barcelona and Parma but Emerson stayed put. He is hopeful his performances alongside Juninho will earn him a belated call-up to the Brazilian national team.

Emerson, seen here during one of his first games for Boro, made a huge impact during the early part of the 1996/97 campaign.

BORO RECORD 1996-

Season	Div	League App	League Gls	Cup App	Cup Gls	Total App	Total Gls
1996/97	P	25	3	9	2	34	5
Total		**25**	**3**	**9**	**2**	**34**	**5**

*Figures correct to 9.4.97

Emerson's darting run and incisive pass set up Juninho's equaliser in this 1-1 draw at Nottingham Forest in August 1996.

Emerson has dual nationality for both Brazil and Portugal and would have the choice of playing for either country if they called upon his services.

MY TOP 5
Emerson

1. Graeme Souness
2. Gary Pallister
3. Juninho
4. Bryan Robson
5. David Armstrong

"He's one of the best midfielders I've ever seen.
The fact that before we bought him nobody had ever heard of him proves how well he's done to now attract the level of attention he does after only a season in England. He's got a lot of people thinking and has proved that Boro are serious about winning things."
Curtis Fleming.

"Emerson is a complete player, he can do everything. He is very good at marking, when he gets the ball he passes it well, he attacks, he defends and he tackles well. Despite his problems, he has done very well for Middlesbrough and if the team does well then I am sure he has a good chance of getting into the Brazil squad He deserves it."
Juninho.

"He is a class act. He's certainly not frightened to lay it about."
Willie Whigham.

"Emerson is a great all-round player. He has great awareness and power and after only a season he is already one of Boro's greats."
Malcolm Allison.

"Emma is still maturing as a player and Middlesbrough fans haven't seen the best of him yet. But once he starts producing on a regular basis the form he showed us when he first came to England, then the fans are going to love him."
Bryan Robson.

"When he first came to Middlesbrough, I thought he was going to be the player of the season. Obviously he then had his problems and his football suffered but the same player is still in there and we've seen flashes of it. He is one of the strongest players I've seen but he has tricks and skills to combine with that strength."
Clayton Blackmore.

"He's a very skilful player but that is combined with hard work and graft."
Trevor Putney.

"He is strong, quick and powerful. It is difficult to cope with the demands of English football but he has shown he could do that regardless of what happened off it. He looks a real handful."
Peter Davenport.

"He's strong but he's also got all the tricks. His all-round play is superb."
Phil Whelan.

"A lot of foreigners don't always look at home in the Premiership but he has settled very well on the pitch for a South American. Every time I have seen him play I have been impressed, he gets stuck in and is very hard to shake off the ball. He also has vision and is a great passer."
Ian Bailey.

"He's a great team player, really strong. Superb on the ball and a great tackler."
Andrew Campbell.

A combination of flair and tenacity made Emerson one of the players to watch during his first season at the Cellnet Riverside Stadium.

John HICKTON

" He was as brave as a lion "

Born: Brimington 24-09-44

Big John, as he was known to the Boro fans, was one of Boro's most prolific goalscorers of the past 30 years.

Stan Anderson signed Hickton from Sheffield Wednesday for a paltry £20,000 in 1966. After progressing through the Hillsborough club's youth ranks as a centre-forward, he was given a defensive role for a spell before returning to his striking duties where he fired home 21 goals in 52 appearances.

On his arrival at Ayresome Park, Hickton initially reverted to his defensive role as a full-back, but as the side struggled in Division Three he was moved forward once again.

He became an instant hit with the fans for the ferocious way he took the side's penalties and he finished the 1966/67 promotion campaign with 17 goals.

Back in Division Two, Hickton became the focal point of Boro's attack, rarely missing a game over the proceeding decade and finishing top scorer every season between 1968 and 1973.

Unfortunately, Hickton was never awarded any international recognition but he did attract interest from several First Division clubs while Boro were in Division Two.

A big, powerful striker with a fine attitude, Hickton was unfortunately in the twilight of his career when the side won the Second Division championship in 1974, but he still managed his quota of goals. Hickton's loyalty was rewarded with a testimonial in 1977 and he played his final game for the club as a substitute at Ipswich Town in 1978.

On leaving Boro, he moved to the NASL with Fort Lauderdale, but unfortunately broke his leg and retired from the professional game soon after his return to English football with Hartlepool, before spending a short spell with non-league Whitby Town. John now lives in the Chesterfield area where he works in the insurance business.

Sporting Boro's famous white-banded shirt of the 70's, John Hickton was popular with players and fans alike.

BORO RECORD 1966-78

Season	Div	League App	League Gls	Cup App	Cup Gls	Total App	Total Gls
1966/67	3	40	15	5	2	45	17
1967/68	2	42	24	8	5	50	29
1968/69	2	34(3)	18	3	0	37(3)	18
1969/70	2	42	24	10	6	52	30
1970/71	2	41	25	5	2	46	27
1971/72	2	39(1)	12	8	4	47(1)	16
1972/73	2	36(2)	13	5	2	41(3)	15
1973/74	2	40	11	4	0	44	11
1974/75	1	39	8	14	3	53	11
1975/76	1	35(1)	9	16	9	51(1)	18
1976/77	1	4(5)	0	0(3)	0	4(8)	0
1977/78	1	3(8)	0	0(3)	0	3(11)	0
Total		**395(20)**	**159**	**78(6)**	**33**	**473(26)**	**192**

John Hickton

Big John challenges QPR's Terry Venables during the early 1970s. In the background is a fellow member of the Boro's Best select - Eric McMordie.

John Hickton was the Second Division's top goalscorer three times... in 1967/68, 1969/70 and 1970/71

"When I began to understand the game more I appreciated just how good John Hickton was. I used to stand on the Holgate End and watch him, his attitude towards scoring goals was tremendous. He was like a god, so much so that I thought I would be embarrassed to bump into him. I've since come across him once or twice in recent years and he's a smashing fella - really down to earth."
Mark Proctor.

"He was my idol as a boy. When I was out playing football in the parks, I always wanted to be John Hickton. To be honest, I don't remember a great deal about him as a player apart from his long run-ups for penalties and that he was a robust player of which there was no better sight than seeing his hair flapping as he belted along and walloped one in."
Tony Mowbray.

"He was the most whole-hearted, brave player I ever had the privilege to play with. When the chips were down, he never let you down and would die for the club. You have to have people who are totally committed to the cause. You can have your skilful individuals but without characters like John Hickton you will struggle. He was also very calm in situations like penalty taking. He would be nerveless."
Malcolm Smith.

MY TOP 5
Willie Whigham

1. John Hickton
2. Juninho
3. Emerson
4. Gordon Jones
5. Willie Maddren

"He was an all-out 100 per cent player. He was the club's top scorer for six or seven seasons. He was unselfish - he made as many as he scored - and very brave - every week he had his head or nose kicked in. Even if you were six down, he would still be trying his hardest."
Stuart Boam.

It's another goal for Big John, one of Boro's all-time favourites.

"John Hickton is what you would describe as an automatic first choice player. He was an all-round player who played at centre-back originally then very well at right-back before moving up front. He scored a tremendous amount of goals and was top scorer for the club for a long time. He had two good feet and he could strike the ball very well while he had the ability to dig the ball out from underneath his feet as he didn't require much back-lift. It surprised me that John never received any international recognition with England because he had the potential for that level. Perhaps because Middlesbrough were in the Second Division when he was at his peak prevented him from winning caps, but he still scored goals in the First Division even when he was moving towards the end of his career."
Stan Anderson.

"He was as brave as a lion and one of the most popular post-war Boro players. He went from being an out and out goalscorer who didn't contribute too much more, into a target man. Jack Charlton almost transformed him. And you knew he would go through a brick wall for you."
Willie Maddren.

"His work-rate was unbelievable. I always made sure he was in my five-a-side team."
Bobby Murdoch.

"He was a workhorse. He wanted to win, was a good goalscorer and worked his socks off. He was a real handful to play against."
Terry Cooper.

MY TOP 5
John Hickton

1. Graeme Souness
2. Willie Maddren
3. David Armstrong
4. Jim Platt
5. John Craggs

"He had a great partnership with David Mills when I was at the club. Hicky was an extremely good header of the ball, very brave, and would put his head into get kicked. He was a smashing lad who always gave 100 per cent."
Jack Charlton.

"Above all, John was a great worker on the pitch . Stan Anderson originally bought him to replace me at centre-back but when I went along to see him, he told me that he was just trying to make me play harder. I couldn't have played harder if I tried! Instead, John moved up front and came into his own with this great burst of speed he possessed. As time went on, he became a very good team worker who would bring players into the game."
Dicky Rooks.

George HARDWICK

" A polished full-back and a gentleman "

Born: Saltburn 02-02-20

Gentleman George provided Boro with inspirational leadership through one of the most successful periods in the club's history. In the post-war years Hardwick captained the team from left-back and was recognised as one of the best defenders of the era.

As a youngster, Hardwick had caught the eye of scouts from Arsenal and Rangers but he set his heart on joining his local club and signed professional forms in 1937 - 18 months after first joining the club as an amateur.

Hardwick's debut in December 1937 gave little indication of what was to follow. The 17-year-old put the ball into his own net in the first minute of a game against Bolton at Ayresome Park. Hardwick managed only a handful of games in the remainder of the season and spent the whole of the 1938-39 season on the sidelines.

During the war years, Hardwick served in the RAF but turned out in two cup finals as a guest for Chelsea and was selected for 17 war-time internationals, all as captain. He also managed to overcome injuries to his legs suffered in an air raid and was in the starting line-up for Boro's first post-war league game.

Hardwick's first goal came from the penalty spot in a cup tie in January 1946 - eight years after his debut. He established himself in the Boro side for the subsequent seasons and earned his first full peace-time England cap against Scotland at Wembley in April 1947. Hardwick wore the captain's armband that day and held on to it every time he pulled on an England shirt. He also starred in and captained the post-war Great Britain side, which played against Europe.

Hardwick ended his playing days with Boro in November 1950 when he opted to move to Oldham Athletic as player-manager after earlier turning down the chance to move to Everton as player-coach. Hardwick steered Oldham to promotion into the Second Division in 1953 but after just a season they dropped back down into the Third and Hardwick resigned in 1956 with the club struggling.

After spells coaching the US Army, PSV Eindhoven and the Dutch FA, Hardwick returned to Ayresome Park in 1961 as youth team coach. He was given his last chance at league management with neighbours Sunderland. Despite leading the club to their highest league position since the war, he was dismissed. Hardwick was given a Boro testimonial in 1983 and is a regular at the Cellnet Riverside Stadium where he has a suite named after him.

George Hardwick: a legend with Boro, England and Great Britain.

BORO RECORD 1937-50

Season	Div	League App	League Gls	Cup App	Cup Gls	Total App	Total Gls
1937/38	1	8	0	2	0	10	0
1945/46	1	0	0	7	2	7	2
1946/47	1	33	1	7	0	40	1
1947/48	1	30	1	3	0	33	1
1948/49	1	39	2	1	0	40	2
1949/50	1	22	0	3	0	25	0
1950/51	1	11	1	0	0	11	1
Total		**143**	**5**	**23**	**2**	**166**	**7**

England: 13 caps (all with Boro) 0 gls.

Hardwick shows the style for England that made him a huge star for club and country.

"He was a classic full-back. As well as being a good tackler, he also never wasted the ball, he always pushed it to his man."
Micky Fenton.

"The best left-back I saw in my time in England."
Alex McCrae.

"A polished full-back and a gentleman."
Dicky Robinson.

"George was a top international while with Boro and in fairness there have not been too many of those so he would have to be alongside Wilf Mannion as my top choices."
Lennie Lawrence.

MY TOP 5
Ronnie Dicks

1. George Hardwick
2. Wilf Mannion
3. Dicky Robinson
4. Micky Fenton
5. Bill Linacre

During World War II, George Hardwick guested for Chelsea and appeared in two FA Cup finals. His manager was former Boro star Billy Birrell.

Two great Boro captains - Hardwick and Tony Mowbray - wave to the fans during a lap of honour at Ayresome Park which saw 60 stars of yesteryear paraded on the pitch before the final match at the ground.

"He was a good full-back and a good captain. He seemed to have that quality of getting a side going. He didn't shout a lot but when he said something, we would do it."
Geoff Walker.

"He was possibly a bit slow on the turn but he read the game so well. He kept many an outside right out of the game including Stanley Matthews. He was also a brilliant captain, very popular, and he led from the front."
Harry Bell.

"I only ever really saw clips of him but he was class. He had a lovely left foot and was one of the greatest ever left-backs. He was also a very good manager when he came to Sunderland but was never given the chance to show what he could do."
Dicky Rooks.

"He was a full-back before his time in the sense that he could get the ball and play it. Normally at that time, they would just get the ball and kick it. He also had charm and to even be in his company gave you confidence. I was coach at Sunderland in his time as manager at Roker Park and to see him walk in the ground gave you a lift."
Brian Clough.

MY TOP 5
George Hardwick

1 Bob Baxter
2 Wilf Mannion
3 Alex McCrae
4 Rolando Ugolini
5 Jimmy Gordon

"Captain of Boro, England and Great Britain - what more can you say? Like me, he was from Lingdale and George achieved so much in the game. He was a very intelligent footballer who I'm sure would have looked outstanding nowadays."
Derek Stonehouse.

"George was full of command and he was always very relaxed. He used to curl the ball up the wing for his team-mates to run on to. And you always knew if you had been hit by a tackle from George!"
Billy Day.

"George was a great reader of the game and gave everybody confidence. He never messed about with the ball when he was passing it back to me, he was always very firm with his passing."
Rolando Ugolini.

"He was a great club man apart from being a first class full-back. He was just the best there was in the country at the time."
Ronnie Dicks.

MY TOP 5
Tom Blenkinsopp

1 George Hardwick
2 Wilf Mannion
3 Stan Anderson
4 Graeme Souness
5 Jimmy Gordon

Fabrizio RAVANELLI

" A world-class finisher "

Born: Perugia 11-12-68

Goal machine Fabrizio Ravanelli amazed many soccer pundits when he left European champions Juventus for Boro during the summer of 1996. His £7m fee smashed the club's previous transfer record but 'Ab Fab' repaid the sum with goals galore, including a stunning hat-trick on his Boro debut against Liverpool.

Although now a feared international striker of the highest calibre, Ravanelli's climb to the top was a long one and he did not make his debut in Italy's Serie A until he was 24 years old. He began his professional playing career in Serie C2 with his hometown club Perugia where his goalscoring exploits (41 goals in 90 league games) earned him a move to Avellino. However, he failed to score for his new club and, after a long loan spell with Casertana, he joined Reggiana where he rediscovered his best form.

Juventus paid £3 million for Ravanelli in 1992 and he continued on the goal trail in Serie A. No less than 53 goals in his final two seasons with Juventus helped the Italian giants clinch the title and the European Champions League (Ravanelli scoring in the 1996 final against Ajax) while he won a regular place in the Italy team.

Nicknamed La Penna Bianca, which translates to the White Feather in English, Ravanelli was an immediate hit in the Premier League and was among the country's top scorers throughout his first season at the club despite constant rumours that he wanted to return to his home country and misguided stories that Manchester United were ready to pay £10 million for his services. His power and passion made him a handful for opposing defenders and he was voted one of the world's greatest strikers by fellow professionals in a 1996 poll carried out by FourFourTwo magazine. His goals also played a major part in Boro's run to Wembley in the Coca-Cola Cup 1997.

Fabrizio Ravanelli sported a skinhead-style crop on the day he signed for Boro.

BORO RECORD 1996-

Season	Div	League App	League Gls	Cup App	Cup Gls	Total App	Total Gls
1996/97	P	28	14	11	13	39	27
Total		**28**	**14**	**11**	**13**	**39**	**27**

*Figures correct to 9.4.97

Salute: Ravanelli and manager Bryan Robson wave to the fans outside the Cellnet Riverside Stadium after the club had announced his £7 million record signing from Juventus.

In 1996/97, Fabrizio Ravanelli became the first Boro player to score three hat-tricks in one season since John O'Rourke 30 years earlier.

"Rav has a great left foot while he can also run with the ball. He has an excellent percentage scoring ratio."
Malcolm Allison.

"A current Italian international centre-forward and part of a Juventus side that had just won the European Cup when he joined Middlesbrough. He would be a success at any club, at any level, because he is a tremendous finisher. As well as scoring goals, he is a good receiver of the ball and brings people into play. He also has a tremendous attitude for the game and is used to working hard, training hard and playing hard."
Bruce Rioch.

MY TOP 5
Fabrizio Ravanelli

1 Juninho
2 Emerson
3 Gianluca Festa
4 Bryan Robson
5 Vladimir Kinder

"Fabrizio is a top striker who, like say Souness, has done it all at the very highest level. He didn't find it easy when he first came to England and had to adapt his football but he has proved himself by the number of goals he has scored. Quite simply, he's a great goalscorer."
Bryan Robson.

"Fabrizio arrived at Middlesbrough at the peak of his career and he deserves his place in my top five because of this. He had just scored the winning goal in the European Champions League final and he's a regular in the Italian national side. He has a great desire to succeed at Middlesbrough."
Jan Fjortoft.

"Fabrizio is a very good goalscorer and I rate his finishing very highly. He is so strong and dangerous in the box. It is difficult for me to compare him with other strikers but he is one of the best around."
Juninho.

"Rav is very strong for his size, strikes a great ball and is good in the air. I would liken him to a quick version of Norman Whiteside, though perhaps Norman had a few other assets to his game. But Rav is a great finisher and there aren't that many around."
Clayton Blackmore.

"Quite simply, he's an international star - that says it all. He has proved himself as a consistent goalscorer at the very top level in Italy and in England. He looks very difficult to mark and will be a handful for any defence."
Simon Coleman.

"Not only is Ravanelli a great goalscorer anywhere near the box but he does a lot of work to help the rest of the team. That's the sort of thing that other players appreciate."
Andrew Campbell.

"He looks world-class. A natural born goalscorer."
Trevor Putney.

"Ravanelli is class. He's a world-class finisher and a great target man who makes time for himself."
Billy Ashcroft.

MY TOP 5
Simon Coleman

1 Gary Pallister
2 Tony Mowbray
3 Stephen Pears
4 Robbie Mustoe
5 Fabrizio Ravanelli

Ab Fab shows the style and lethal left foot that saw him crack more than 25 goals in his first season in English football.

Bobby MURDOCH

" One of the great visionaries "

Born: Bothwell 17-08-44

Jack Charlton only signed one player in his first season as Middlesbrough manager and he was a free transfer. But Bobby Murdoch proved to be an inspirational buy, playing a crucial role in steering the club into the First Division with his elegant passing.

Murdoch was thought to have his best days behind him when he joined Boro. A successful career with Scottish giants, Celtic, spanning 14 years, began when Murdoch moved to Parkhead from Cambuslang Rangers in 1959. The midfielder helped Celtic to seven consecutive Scottish League titles in the 1960s as well as five wins in each of the two cup competitions. He also played when Celtic became the first British club to win the European Cup in 1967.

Murdoch's first Scottish cap came against Wales in 1966 and his 12th and last in 1970. In 1969, he was voted Scotland's player of the year.

But when Jack Charlton took over as Boro boss, he swooped to take Murdoch to Ayresome Park. Murdoch, then 29, joined Boro on a free transfer in the summer of 1973. He made his Boro debut against Bristol City in September of that year and capped his performance with a goal. With Murdoch in the side, Boro went on to secure promotion into the top flight.

After helping Boro to cement their place in the top flight, Murdoch ended his playing days for Boro in 1975 but stayed on to coach the club's juniors. And after six years in the backroom staff, Murdoch took over the managerial reigns on the departure of John Neal in 1981.

His only full season in charge saw the club relegated to the Second Division and a 4-1 defeat against Grimsby early in the following season signalled the end of Murdoch's reign and the culmination of a nine year association with the club. He now spends his Saturdays as a matchday host at Parkhead.

Bobby Murdoch served the club as player, coach and manager over nine years.

BORO RECORD 1973-76

Season	Div	League App	League Gls	Cup App	Cup Gls	Total App	Total Gls
1973/74	2	33(1)	5	5	0	38(1)	5
1974/75	1	39	1	10	1	49	2
1975/76	1	21(1)	0	14(1)	2	35(2)	2
Total		**93(2)**	**6**	**29(1)**	**3**	**122(3)**	**9**

Scotland: 12 caps (0 with Boro) 5 gls.

Murdoch rises for a header during the opening day clash against Tottenham in August 1975.

"Along with Johnny Haynes and Pat Crerand, Bobby was one of the great visionaries of his era. He could hit perfect 50 yard passes and I would wonder "How the hell did he know he was there?" He was such a good passer of the ball and a very classy player."
Alf Wood.

"He was a great footballer. He was one of the major players that made Middlesbrough into a top flight team with Big Jack. He carried that on behind the scenes when he stopped playing."
David Hodgson.

"All the lads liked Bobby, they admired his ability and skill. He was very knowledgeable about the game. I signed him on a free transfer and I was delighted with what he did. We had a good few years out of him."
Jack Charlton.

Club chairman Charles Amer gave Bobby Murdoch the chance to make his mark as a manager at the start of the 1981/82 season. Sadly, it all ended in tears. Here, the pair discuss plans for the ill-fated campaign during a pre-season photo-call at Ayresome Park.

MY TOP 5 Bobby Murdoch

1 Stuart Boam
2 Graeme Souness
3 David Armstrong
4 Willie Maddren
5 John Hickton

"It was a testing period for the club when Jack Charlton took over and one of the major influences on the success was Bobby Murdoch. He was a big influence on the younger players and his work on the playing side was amazing."
Colin Todd.

"For a free transfer buy he's the best I've ever seen - top class. I'm biased because he coached me when I was a junior but he was a great fella and even though he was finished and out of shape he was still a class act."
Kelham O'Hanlon.

"As a boy I supported Celtic and I watched him then. When he later came to Middlesbrough it was brilliant for me. The first time he played was in a reserve game against Halifax and for me to be in the same team was unbelievable. He was a big influence on me and a lot of the younger players coming through."
Tony McAndrew.

MY TOP 5 Jack Charlton

1 Bobby Murdoch
2 Willie Maddren
3 David Armstrong
4 Graeme Souness
5 John Hickton

"He was coming to the end of his career when he joined Middlesbrough but he had more medals under his kitchen table than most of us will ever see. He wasn't the type of player to run around a lot but he was an extremely good user of the ball."
Stuart Boam.

"If you were looking for a player to play a 30, 40 or 50 yard pass then Bobby was your man, he was spot on with his passing. I was always told that a good player was one who found time to perform his techniques leisurely and that was Bobby. He always found time and was never flustered."
Frank Spraggon.

"Like me, he had his best years before coming to Boro but you could see what a good player he was. He had his weight problems but he was a superb passer."
Terry Cooper.

John HENDRIE

" Strong, quick and skilful "

Born: Lennoxtown 24-10-63

Diminutive Scotsman John Hendrie came to Middlesbrough after spending the previous three seasons with three different clubs. But the winger-cum-striker put aside any assumption that he was a journeyman footballer by loyally serving the club for six years and becoming one of the most popular players in recent times.

Hendrie started his career as an apprentice at Coventry and the Scotland youth player turned pro in 1981. He started just 15 games in three seasons at Highfield Road and was loaned out to Hereford at the back end of the 1983/84 season. In the summer of 1984, Hendrie was on his way and signed for Bradford, then in the old Third Division, on a free transfer. As a regular over four seasons at Valley Parade, he help Bradford win promotion to the Second Division in his first season and was a regular scorer when he caught the eye of Newcastle boss Willie McFaul.

Hendrie made the switch to St James' Park but it was just one season spent in the First Division at Newcastle that ended in relegation and he was on his way to Leeds United. A more successful season followed at Elland Road which saw the club win the Second Division and promotion into the top flight. But Howard Wilkinson decided not to hang on to his tricky winger and Colin Todd brought Hendrie to Ayresome Park for £500,000.

Over the coming seasons, Hendrie switched to a central striking role and established himself as a firm favourite with the fans. He cemented his reputation by scoring the last ever goal at Ayresome Park and was crucial in promotions in 1992 and 1995, finishing as top scorer in the latter campaign and rarely missing a game. He will also be long remembered for what many claim to be Boro's best ever goal - a run from the edge of his own box against Millwall in 1990. In October 1996 he left Boro to join First Division Barnsley for £250,000 where he continued to find the net with regularity.

Hendrie in action during the 1995/96 season, his last full term as a Boro player.

BORO RECORD 1990-96

Season	Div	League App	League Gls	Cup App	Cup Gls	Total App	Total Gls
1990/91	2	40(1)	3	11(1)	1	51(2)	5
1991/92	2	38	3	10(1)	2	48(1)	5
1992/93	P	31(1)	9	5	0	36(1)	9
1993/94	1	27(1)	14	6	5	33(1)	19
1994/95	1	38(2)	15	4	2	42(2)	17
1995/96	P	7(6)	1	1(1)	0	8(7)	1
1996/97	P	0(1)	0	1(1)	0	1(2)	0
Total		**181(12)**	**45**	**38(4)**	**11**	**219(16)**	**56**

Sharp-shooter: Hendrie was Boro's leading scorer as he fired the club to the First Division championship in 1995.

"Hendrie was a better player and a better striker than a lot of people gave him credit for. He was very unlucky not to play for Scotland. In fact, I'm sure if John Hendrie at his best joined the big name Boro side now, he would be a regular in the Scotland set-up. You always knew that if you put the ball to his feet, he wouldn't lose it. He was strong, quick and skilful."
Michael Barron.

"He's a great player. He's scored so many important goals and was a real bargain buy."
Steve Vickers.

John Hendrie scored the last ever goals in competitive action at Ayresome Park. He struck twice in the 2-1 win over Luton Town on April 30 1995.

"He was an all-round excellent player. Whether he was playing on the wing or up the middle, you could always rely on John to produce the goods for the team."
Robbie Mustoe.

"He was committed to the club 100 per cent and a good goalscorer over a long period of time."
Alan Foggon.

"John was another bargain buy in the Slaven mould. Not only was he incredibly consistent, he also scored some real wonder goals for the team. His loyalty to the club also marks him out as something you don't see too much of these days."
Curtis Fleming.

Celebration time in the dressing-room at Molineux in May 1992 after Boro had clinched promotion to the Premier League. John Hendrie leads the party, watched by two more of Boro's Best - Stuart Ripley and Bernie Slaven.

"John had been about a bit when he joined Boro and he turned out to be just the sort of player I like. He was a strong player who could hold the ball up and he has that all important change of pace which reminded him of me in some respects. John has the ability to play wide and down the middle and is a player who always catches the eye."
Terry Cochrane.

"I played against him many times and he was always a pain in the neck to mark. He spent the best years of his career with Middlesbrough."
Nigel Pearson.

"John is a great pro who is still very highly regarded by everyone at Middlesbrough Football Club. He did well for the club over a number of years and established a great rapport with the fans - and rightly so. He's a tireless worker and very hard to dispossess."
Viv Anderson.

"John was one of Middlesbrough's best ever signings. He was superb during my time at the Boro and was loved by everyone at the club and the public."
Alan Miller.

MY TOP 5
John Hendrie

1. **Graeme Souness**
2. **Juninho**
3. **John Hickton**
4. **Brian Clough**
5. **Wilf Mannion**

"Hendrie was so hard to play against and you never knew what he was going to do. He was one of those players who would miss when you expected him to score and score when you thought he had no chance. He also put himself about, as good strikers should. In my book, he's still good enough to be in the Middlesbrough team now. He was a one-off."
Clayton Blackmore.

"I've seen the video clips of Hendrie playing for Middlesbrough two or three years ago and it is clear he was a super striker and very dangerous. He scored some great goals. I wish I could have played with him more."
Mikkel Beck.

"Having played with him for five years I know what a good player he is and what he meant to people at Middlesbrough."
Paul Wilkinson.

Bill HARRIS

" The best passer of the ball I've ever seen "

Born: Swansea 31-10-28

Welsh wizard Bill Harris stood firmly in the Boro side for a decade. The wing-half was renowned for his excellent distribution, laying on many of Brian Clough's huge tally of goals, and it is surprising that his performances for Boro only brought on a handful of international caps.

Harris started his career at his hometown club Swansea City, but failed to impress and was released. He dropped down into the Southern League to join Llanelli but his career outside the League was short-lived as Harris was persuaded to move to England to join Hull City. The Tigers paid out £2,000 for their new signing in March 1950 and the then Division Two side got four years service out of him before he moved up into the top flight to join Middlesbrough for £15,000.

Unfortunately for Harris, his top flight career was only to last nine games. Just a few months after he joined the club, Boro were relegated, not to see the First Division again until after Harris had played the last of almost 400 games for the club.

Harris was given his debut in March 1954 in a 3-3 draw with Chelsea but his efforts failed to save the club from relegation. At previous clubs, Harris had played at wing-half but was converted to inside-forward at Boro with great success and he was a mainstay of the Boro team under Bob Dennison as the team regularly challenged in the top half of the Second Division.

Just two months after joining Boro, Harris received his first international call-up, making his debut in a 2-0 defeat against Austria. The cap was bad news for his old club Hull who had to pay £250 to Llanelli, part of the original deal that had taken Harris to Boothferry Park. Harris spent three years in the international wilderness before being recalled by Wales in 1957. He went on to collect six caps.

Harris left Boro and moved to Bradford City as player-manager in March 1965. But after an unsuccessful year in Division Four, he returned to Teesside to manage Stockton. He died in 1989.

He may not be one of the club's best-known names but Bill Harris was highly rated by all who saw him play.

BORO RECORD 1954-65

Season	Div	League App	League Gls	Cup App	Cup Gls	Total App	Total Gls
1953/54	1	9	1	0	0	9	1
1954/55	2	41	1	1	0	42	1
1955/56	2	42	1	2	0	44	1
1956/57	2	42	8	3	1	45	9
1957/58	2	39	3	2	0	41	3
1958/59	2	36	7	1	0	37	7
1959/60	2	35	11	1	0	36	11
1960/61	2	31	7	1	0	32	7
1961/62	2	30	14	4	1	34	15
1962/63	2	15	2	1	0	16	2
1963/64	2	34	11	1	1	35	12
1964/65	2	6	3	1	0	7	3
Total		**360**	**69**	**18**	**3**	**378**	**72**

Wales: 6 caps (all with Boro) 0 gls.

Class of 54/55: Harris (back row, third right) with his Boro team-mates at Ayresome Park. Rolando Ugolini (back row, second right) and Dicky Robinson (back row, far right) are two fellow members of the Boro's Best select line-up.

"Bill was a wing-half, you could compare him to Franz Beckenbauer. He was always so relaxed. He wasn't a heavy tackler but when you were on top he was complete class, controlling the game."
Billy Day.

Bill Harris could stroll through the game, he was the proverbial stroller. His passing ability made him. I remember when I was playing in the reserves at Halifax as a youngster and we won 11-0. Bill set up every single goal and I remember him most for that game alone."
Frank Spraggon.

"Bill was at the end of his career when I played for the club but he was still quality then. He had been skipper for many years and that speaks volumes. He must have been a hell of a good player when he was at his peak because his distribution and control in the middle still made him a very good player when he was 36 years old."
Mel Nurse.

"He was the best passer of the ball I have ever seen. He would be worth a lot of money if he was playing today. I remember seeing him play in a game against Johnny Giles and it was a joy to watch them both in action."
Billy Horner.

"Bill had the ability to see things quicker. There is more to being a professional footballer than passing the ball from A to B, you've got to be able to read situations and have skill. Bill was similar to Juninho in that respect. He could control the ball, pass and read the game. He was a great influence on the younger players because he was so well respected."
Gordon Jones.

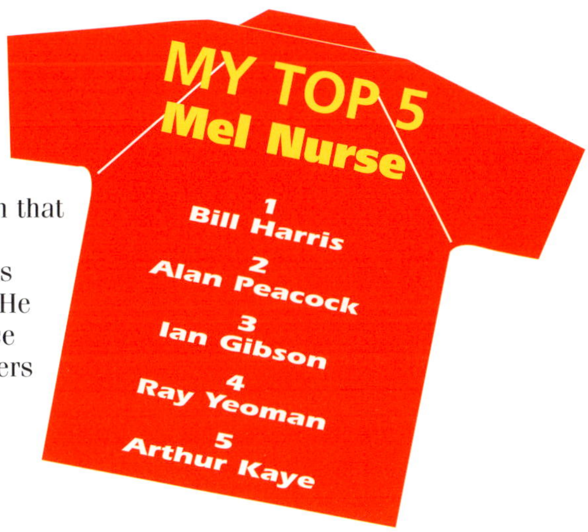

May 1960 and Boro pose for a picture outside Middlesbrough railway station before an end-of-season tour to Germany. Members of Boro's Best are Gordon Jones (second left), Bill Harris (third left), Jimmy Gordon (sixth left), Micky Fenton (fourth right) and Brian Clough (far right).

"He was probably the finest wing-half and passer of the ball I ever saw. He could do everything but head the ball. For all the goals Clough scored, he made most of them."
Bryan Phillips.

MY TOP 5
Gordon Jones

1. Bill Harris
2. Graeme Souness
3. Hugh McIlmoyle
4. Juninho
5. Alan Peacock

"Bill had such good skills and he was ever so cool on the ball. He was also very intelligent and clever with the ball. When I played behind him, he often sold the man he was attacking a dummy and sold me one as well."
Ray Bilcliff.

"He was always very constructive and had a good eye for the ball. The only thing that let him down were his defensive qualities - he didn't have any. But he was so good on the ball, it would just flow to you."
Alan Peacock.

MY TOP 5
Bryan Phillips

1. Wilf Mannion
2. Bill Harris
3. Brian Clough
4. Mick McNeil
5. Edwin Holliday

Craig JOHNSTON

" Craig was a one-off "

Born: Johannesburg 08-01-60

The canny Australian Craig Johnston could never be accused of giving up too easily. It took two expensive flights from the other side of the world to persuade Boro that he was worth a contract. But the club got its reward in one of the hardest working players ever to have pulled on a Boro shirt and Johnston went on to build a hugely successful football career.

South African-born Johnston grew up in Australia and wrote to Boro for a trial after seeing the club playing on tour in New South Wales. He paid his own way to fly over to England but Jack Charlton decided against keeping the midfield dynamo. But Johnston's persistence paid off when he was offered a second trial by the club's new manager John Neal in 1977. He made another mammoth journey from Australia and this time impressed enough to be signed.

In the week leading up to his Boro debut, Johnston was involved in a dramatic sea rescue while swimming in the Channel. But he was fit to take the field against Everton in the FA Cup in January 1978. His impressive performances in the Boro midfield soon came to the attention of international managers and he opted for England over Scotland and Australia for his international hopes and won two under-21 caps. In a whirlwind three-year career with Boro, Johnston managed less than a hundred appearances for the club. Playing at number four, Johnston notched up 10 goals from midfield in his final season with the club and earned himself a move to the reigning league champions Liverpool in April 1981 for £580,000.

After seven successful seasons with Liverpool, Johnston surprisingly retired at the age of 27 and returned to his native Australia to nurse his ill sister. After a spell as a journalist he then proved his eye for opportunity once again with the design of the successful Adidas Predator football boot.

Sporting the name of Boro's first sponsors, Datsun Cleveland, Craig Johnston is pictured in August 1980.

BORO RECORD 1977-81

Season	Div	League App	Gls	Cup App	Gls	Total App	Gls
1977/78	1	4(1)	1	2(2)	0	6(3)	1
1978/79	1	1(1)	0	0(2)	0	1(3)	0
1979/80	1	29(1)	5	3	0	32(1)	5
1980/81	1	27	10	5	0	32	10
Total		**61(3)**	**16**	**10(4)**	**0**	**71(7)**	**16**

Johnston was affectionately nicknamed Roo by his team-mates.

MY TOP 5
Jan Fjortoft

1. Graeme Souness
2. Gary Pallister
3. Fabrizio Ravanelli
4. Bryan Robson
5. Craig Johnston

"Craig was a one-off, he would run for miles. I played him in centre midfield with Mark Proctor and let him loose. With Proctor and David Armstrong alongside him he was able to get away with it but his work-rate was unbelievable. After 25 minutes, he would get a second wind, and then after 50 he would get a third wind and then a fourth after 75 minutes. He was very genuine. He was one of the few players I would have to bring off the training field because he would have stayed there all day and done damage to himself."
John Neal.

Johnston challenges for possession during a game with Wolves in the 1980/81 season, his last at Ayresome Park.

"He was one of the players I admired when I was watching from the terraces as a lad. His work-rate was phenomenal and he was very skilful as well. He was committed to the cause and the fans appreciated that."
Stuart Ripley.

" A very athletic player who was also quite skilful and could score goals. Craig went onto fulfil his potential at Liverpool."
Lennie Lawrence.

" Right from when he was a kid and his dad paid for him to come over for a trial, what he achieved was all down to himself. He came over as a scrawny lad and didn't have a great deal going for him but I have never seen anyone work as hard as him to get what he wanted. He was the first one in every day, practising on the car park and would even take the ball home with him."
Ian Bailey.

"You've got to respect the achievements of Craig Johnston with Liverpool but he learned his trade with Middlesbrough. You must also respect what he has achieved after football and the way he got himself into football at Middlesbrough. He was very self-minded."
Jan Fjortoft.

"Johnston's story, paying his own way to Boro from Australia and being rejected, was the stuff dreams are made of and he made you proud to be a Boro supporter. He was obviously always a natural athlete but worked hard on his game to become a top class player as well."
Lee Turnbull.

"He was a fantastic athlete from box to box. He was slightly extravagant with his flowing locks and scored spectacular goals. Like all the best Boro players at the time, it was inevitable a big club would come along and take him away."
Peter Beagrie.

"Craig was the fittest guy I've ever seen and he was so committed. He used to be at the Hutton Road training ground at six o'clock in the morning, kicking a ball against a wall. It was his commitment that got him to the top with Liverpool because, although he did have natural ability, he had to work on it in a similar way to Kevin Keegan. When he first arrived at the club he was a bit of a joke but I've never seen anybody so determined and he soon proved himself with the lads."
Graham Hedley.

"Johnston was quick, had lovely control and loved taking defenders on - that's what the fans liked about him and players appreciated those skills too. He was a team player and linked up with team-mates so well."
Brian Laws.

"Although he didn't have the longest career, what impressed me about him was his determination. He made himself into a player and ended up moving to one of the biggest clubs around. When he came to the club he wasn't really wanted but he worked hard and was determined to make it."
Mick Burns.

Craig Johnston was less than two months past his 17th birthday when he made his first team debut in a 3-2 FA Cup win over Everton in January 1979. He remains Boro's youngest ever FA Cup player.

Bryan ROBSON

" There can't be too many better players who have pulled on the Boro shirt "

Born: Witton Gilbert 11-01-57

A player who was 37 years old when he moved to Boro and whose appearances number only a quarter of a century may seem an unlikely choice among Boro's Best, but Bryan Robson's influence on the club is immeasurable. An illustrious career that reached all the heights may have been in its twilight days but Robson's arrival signalled the start of a revolution at Middlesbrough.

Bryan Robson started his career at West Bromwich Albion in 1974. He swiftly added England under-21 caps to his England Youth record while with the Baggies before his former WBA manager Ron Atkinson paid a British record fee of £1.5 million to take him to Manchester United in 1981.

In 13 seasons at Old Trafford, as Captain Marvel and inspirational midfield general, Robson built a reputation as one of England's greatest players. He captained the side throughout his time at the club as United challenged for honours on all fronts including three FA Cup victories and a European Cup Winners' Cup triumph. After twice finishing as runners-up in the First Division, Robson finally saw the club achieve its dream of the league title in each of his last two years with the club.

The first of a phenomenal 90 caps for England came while still with West Brom in 1980 but he was a regular throughout the 1980s, only missing out on a century of appearances through a long list of injuries that included three broken legs and a repeatedly dislocated shoulder. He was forced to return home early from two World Cup Final competitions in 1986 and 1990. The injuries also prevented Robson adding even further to the 700 plus games he played in his professional career.

At the start of the 1994/95 season, Robson was persuaded to leave Old Trafford to join Second Division Middlesbrough. Chairman Steve Gibson brought in Robson to help mastermind his dream of making Boro into one of England's top clubs. He played more than 20 games as player-manager in his first season with the Boro, helping to steer the club into the Premier League at the first attempt in time for the move to the Cellnet Riverside Stadium. He has since been an infrequent sight as a player but became the oldest star in the Premier League and Boro's oldest ever player when he took to the field against Arsenal just 10 days short of his 40th birthday on New Year's Day 1997.

He may have won 90 caps as an England player but Robson was also a success as a coach for his country. He is seen here in his role as assistant to Terry Venables in the build-up to Euro 96.

BORO RECORD 1994-

Season	Div	League App	Gls	Cup App	Gls	Total App	Gls
1994/95	1	21(1)	1	0	0	21(1)	1
1995/96	P	1(1)	0	2	0	3(1)	0
1996/97	P	1	0	0	0	1	0
Total		**23(2)**	**1**	**2**	**0**	**25(2)**	**1**

England: 90 caps (none with Boro) 26 gls.

Robson in action in his role as player-manager during the 1994/95 title-winning season.

Boro beat a host of other clubs to acquire the services of Bryan Robson in May 1994. Robbo was also wanted by Coventry, Wolves, Aston Villa and Sheffield Wednesday.

Bryan Robson

"I saw him play more for Manchester United than for Middlesbrough when I used to watch English football on TV in Brazil. He is a similar player to Emerson in that he can win the ball and then use it well. He can mark, tackle, pass and get forward. He scored a lot of goals for Manchester United and, although he was in his late thirties when he joined Middlesbrough, he was still a very good player."
Juninho.

"I would pick him simply for who he is and what he has achieved at Middlesbrough. He played in the team himself to start with and there can't be too many better players who have pulled on the Boro shirt."
Colin Cooper.

"He hasn't played many games but for ability and know-how he's the best I've seen. It was just great to watch him train."
Ian Johnson.

"I would pick him for what he did at Manchester United and for the sheer effort he puts into every game he plays."
Chris Morris.

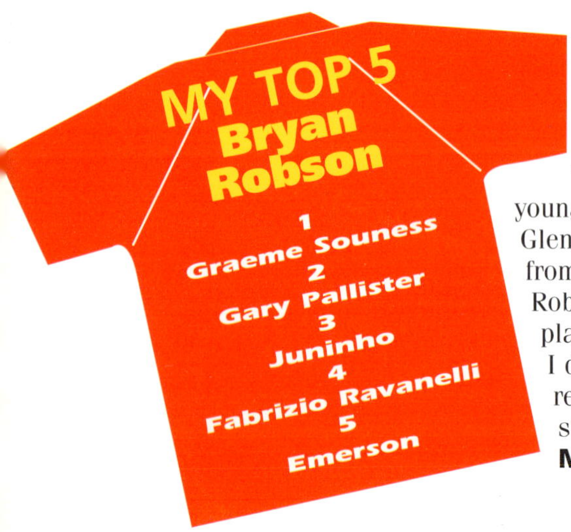

"When I was a youngster my idol was Glenn Hoddle who was from the same era as Robbo but when you played against Robbo, as I did for Boro, you realise what a really strong player he was."
Mark Burke.

Robbo and club captain Nigel Pearson lift the 1995 Football League championship trophy on the pitch at Ayresome Park.

Bob BAXTER

" An inspirational player and a great centre-half "

Born: Gilmerton 23-01-11

It was a stroke of luck that brought Scotsman Bob Baxter to Middlesbrough in 1932. Boro manager Peter McWilliam had travelled to Scotland to keep tabs on a player he was considering bringing to the club. But the game was called off and, rather than return to Teesside, McWilliam called in to see Bruntonian Juniors and spotted Baxter. Boro had reason to bless their fortune when Baxter developed into a fine player and an inspirational captain.

Baxter turned his back on a sideline running a dance band when he moved to Teesside and made his debut for the club against Birmingham in October 1932. Over the following seasons, Baxter played in nine different positions but settled in a central defensive role on the departure of centre-half and captain Tom Griffiths. Baxter took on the pivotal role at the back and assumed the captaincy.

He won his first cap for Scotland in November 1938 against Wales, settling in alongside the future Liverpool manager Bill Shankly in the centre of defence. He won three caps, his last against England in April 1939, and would surely have won many more had it not been for the outbreak of war later that year.

War also disrupted Baxter's Boro career. He was 28 when fighting started and returned to Scotland to work in the mines and run a newsagent and tabacconist shop. He also guested for Hibernian and Hearts and played in four war-time internationals. By the time league football returned, Baxter had been released by Boro and joined Hearts. He later returned to the Teesside area in his retirement before his death.

Bobby Baxter was a stalwart pre-war centre-back - and the hero of George Hardwick.

BORO RECORD 1932-39

Season	Div	League App	Gls	Cup App	Gls	Total App	Gls
1932/33	1	25	5	4	1	29	6
1933/34	1	36	6	2	0	38	6
1934/35	1	39	6	1	0	40	6
1935/36	1	39	2	4	0	43	2
1936/37	1	37	0	1	0	38	0
1937/38	1	38	0	3	0	41	0
1938/39	1	33	0	4	0	37	0
Total		**247**	**19**	**19**	**1**	**266**	**20**

Scotland: 3 caps (all with Boro) 0 gls.

"When he first arrived at Middlesbrough he was playing as an inside-forward but when the club was hit with a problem at centre-half Bob moved there. He did so well at centre-half that he was picked and eventually captained Scotland. A good footballer, he was exceptionally strong for a man who was not very tall for a centre-half, just 5'10". When I was a youngster coming through into the Boro team Bob was great with me, he was an inspirational sort of player and also a natural comedian!"
George Hardwick.

MY TOP 5
Harold Shepherdson

1. Bob Baxter
2. Micky Fenton
3. George Camsell
4. George Hardwick
5. Wilf Mannion

"I didn't see much of Baxter because I was only young as his career was coming to an end but he used to obliterate star strikers from the visiting teams at Ayresome Park. Boro have been lucky enough to have had two or three good centre-halves but Baxter was more versatile than most."
Derek Stonehouse.

MY TOP 5
George Hardwick

1. Bob Baxter
2. Wilf Mannion
3. Alex McCrae
4. Rolando Ugolini
5. Jimmy Gordon

"A great centre-half, very good in the air and a great tackler."
Alex McCrae.

Baxter wins this challenge with Mills of Chelsea at Stamford Bridge in January 1937 but his opponent had the last laugh - Chelsea won 1-0.

Robbie MUSTOE

" A players' player and hard worker"

Born: Oxford 28-08-68

It is a credit to Robbie Mustoe that a player who joined a Middlesbrough side which had narrowly avoided dropping into the old Third Division still commands a first team place amongst the all-star line-up of today. A £375,000 buy from Oxford United during the summer of 1990, Mustoe's loyalty and ever-improving displays make him one of the club's all-time bargains.

A hard-working midfield ball-winner, Mustoe delayed his professional career to study computing at college as a youngster but won his first team chance for hometown club Oxford against Liverpool in 1987 in the old First Division. Sadly, United were relegated soon afterwards but Mustoe quickly won a regular place in the side, scoring seven league goals in his final season at the Manor Ground and earning a call-up into the England under-21 squad.

Few Boro fans knew much about Mustoe when then manager Colin Todd signed him for the start of the 1990/91 season but two memorable goals in a Rumbelows Cup win over North-east rivals Newcastle United did much to win over the supporters. He remained a regular in the side under Todd's successor, Lennie Lawrence, playing his part in the 1992 promotion success and the club's run to the semi-final of the Rumbelows Cup. Then, after initially being left out, he earned a place in the new-look Boro side under Bryan Robson in 1994, though injury ruled him out of the promotion run-in, as it had done two years earlier.

In the Premier League, Mustoe has been one of Boro's most consistent performers in his midfield holding role. Vastly under-rated, he is a players' player who has become a fans' favourite too. His never-say-die attitude and willingness to run all day have made him a vital cog in the Boro machine, while the tricky skills of team-mate Juninho have also rubbed off on him.

Robbie Mustoe in typical action, this time against Tottenham at the Cellnet Riverside Stadium in October 1996.

BORO RECORD 1990-

Season	Div	League App	League Gls	Cup App	Cup Gls	Total App	Total Gls
1990/91	2	39(2)	4	11(1)	3	50(3)	7
1991/92	2	28(2)	2	13(1)	1	41(3)	3
1992/93	P	21(2)	1	2	0	23(2)	1
1993/94	1	39	2	11	2	50	4
1994/95	1	26(3)	3	6	1	32(3)	4
1995/96	P	21	1	3	1	24	2
1996/97	P	25	2	11	0	36	2
Total		**199(9)**	**15**	**46(2)**	**9**	**256(11)**	**23**

*Figures correct to 9.4.97

Mustoe charges through the Liverpool defence during the 3-3 home draw on the opening day of the 1996/97 campaign.

"I think Robbie is different from many other English players because he has such good technique. He tackles and wins the ball for you but then he knows what to do with it, where to pass it and always passes simply but well. He is a good player to have in your team."
Juninho.

"Players have come and gone over the years but Robbie is still there and going strong. He's not a big name like some others but he has a key role despite the fact that Middlesbrough are now a team full of international stars. He's a players' player. Anyway, I had to vote for him - I was his best man!"
Simon Coleman.

MY TOP 5
Robbie Mustoe

1 Tony Mowbray
2 Stephen Pears
3 John Hendrie
4 Bernie Slaven
5 Stuart Ripley

"Robbie is a hard-working, 100 per cent player who I have a lot of respect for. He's a players' player."
Craig Hignett.

"Robbie never gets the praise he deserves. He gets through an immense amount of work in the midfield but rarely does he get the glory. He's a players' player."
Steve Vickers.

"He's a vastly under-rated player in the Souness mould. Robbie gets through so much work in midfield but is also capable of putting his foot on the ball and playing the game the way it should be played. It's always nice to have a team full of flair but you will always need the Robbie Mustoe's of this world."
Alan Miller.

"He always maintains consistency on the pitch. You always know you have strength behind you and you can take any team on with Robbie on your shoulder."
Jamie Pollock.

"A good player and a hard worker. He keeps it nice and simple and can weigh in with a few goals."
Andy Todd.

Micky FENTON

"Had all the attributes of a top goalscorer"

Born: Stockton 30-10-13

Centre-forward Micky Fenton sits proudly in Boro's all-time top five goalscorers with an impressive tally of 162 goals from 269 games. And had the long-serving one-club player not lost six seasons to the Second World War, he would surely have added even further to his excellent record.

The Teesside youngster joined Boro as a professional in March 1933. He made his debut in a 4-0 win over Blackburn in the last game of the 1932/33 season alongside George Camsell in attack. He gave an indication of what was to come by netting in that game and it was the goalscoring legend Camsell whose mantle Fenton eventually assumed, after a couple of seasons as an infrequent selection. As Camsell's career came to a close, Fenton became top scorer for each of the last three seasons before the outbreak of war, including 34 goals in 33 games as Boro challenged for the title in 1938/39.

Fenton continued to guest for Boro in the war years and played in one international to complement the only official England cap he had earned in 1938 against Scotland at Wembley.

By the time football resumed Fenton had reached the age of 33 but he proved he could still play at the top level by regularly finding the net once again. He finished as top scorer in each of the three seasons after the war to mirror his pre-war achievements. The last of the trio, the 1948/49 season, saw him come out on top despite only playing 24 games.

Everton had attempted to sign Fenton as a replacement for the departed Tommy Lawton in October 1946 but he opted to remain at Ayresome Park to play out the rest of his career. His last game came as an emergency stand-in against Aston Villa in January 1950 - almost 17 years after his debut - at the age of 36. He had already moved into the club's backroom staff and was involved with the reserves. He was a coach at the club into the mid-1960s. He still lives in the Stockton area and is a regular at the Cellnet Riverside Stadium.

Micky Fenton wearing the famous pre-war Boro shirt.

BORO RECORD 1932-50

Season	Div	League App	League Gls	Cup App	Cup Gls	Total App	Total Gls
1932/33	1	1	1	0	0	1	1
1933/34	1	3	0	0	0	3	0
1934/35	1	21	8	1	0	22	8
1935/36	1	6	0	3	0	9	0
1936/37	1	35	22	1	0	36	22
1937/38	1	36	24	3	2	39	26
1938/39	1	33	34	4	1	37	35
1945/46	1	-	-	7	7	7	7
1946/47	1	40	18	7	5	47	23
1947/48	1	40	28	2	0	42	28
1948/49	1	24	12	1	0	25	12
1949/50	1	1	0	0	0	1	0
Total		**240**	**147**	**29**	**15**	**269**	**162**

England: 1 cap (with Boro) 0 gls.

But for the intervention of the Second World War, Micky Fenton would undoubtedly have won more than one England cap.

"He was in the Hughie Gallacher mould. He wasn't the tallest man, he was small for a centre-forward, but he had a sharpness about him and all the attributes of a top goalscorer."
Brian Clough.

"He was one of those lads who had a knack of scoring goals. He led the line well and did exactly what he was picked for. He wasn't a physical man but he had plenty of playing strengths."
Ronnie Dicks.

"I played when Micky was at the back end of his career but he was still a great centre-forward. He hit the ball very hard, was good in the air and was fast and intelligent. In those days it was man-to-man marking and Micky was good at getting out of the road to make space for others."
Harry Bell.

"Micky was a natural goalscorer."
Geoff Walker.

Alan PEACOCK

"A great leader of the line and lethal in the air"

Born: Middlesbrough 29-10-37

Peacock was half of one of Boro's most successful strike forces alongside goalscoring legend Brian Clough. The pair formed a formidable partnership with Peacock's power in the air allied to Clough's lethal finishing. And, after Clough's departure, Peacock became a top goalscorer in his own right and an England striker despite never playing for Boro in the top flight.

Peacock joined Boro in November 1954 but had to wait a year to make his debut. He came in against Bristol Rovers but with the game ending in a 7-2 defeat, he had to wait four months for another chance. He scored his first two goals later that season in a 4-2 win over Nottingham Forest. National Service disrupted his early playing career, but after being picked for the England Youth team, Peacock took a firm hold on the striking place alongside Clough mid-way through the 1957/58 season. In the last 17 games of the season, the pair scored 31 goals between them and a lethal partnership was born.

Although Clough consistently outscored Peacock over the next three seasons, Peacock's contribution was outstanding. The pair comfortably outscored their team-mates including the rare feat of both scoring hat-tricks in a 6-1 win over Scunthorpe in November 1958.

Clough beat Peacock to England honours but once his strike partner had moved on to Sunderland, Peacock came into his own, netting 24 goals in 34 games in 1961/62 and earning a place in the squad for the 1962 World Cup Finals in Chile, overcoming a knee injury which had threatened to rule him out, to play against Argentina and Bulgaria. More caps followed after the tournament, including a 4-0 win over Wales when Peacock scored twice.

Injury severely disrupted the 1963/64 season and in February 1964 he joined Leeds in a £55,000 deal - a club record sale that was to stand for 14 years. He won a Second Division championship medal and played in a cup final with his new club, also adding two more caps before moving on to Plymouth. He was forced to retire in 1968, aged 30, with a knee injury. He lives in the Middlesbrough area and is a match-day host at the Cellnet Riverside Stadium.

Alan Peacock was very much a player's player, greatly appreciated by his team-mates in Boro's colours.

BORO RECORD 1955-64

Season	Div	League App	League Gls	Cup App	Cup Gls	Total App	Total Gls
1955/56	2	6	2	0	0	6	2
1956/57	2	4	1	0	0	4	1
1957/58	2	22	15	2	2	24	17
1958/59	2	34	19	1	0	35	19
1959/60	2	35	13	1	0	36	13
1960/61	2	34	15	2	1	36	16
1961/62	2	34	24	7	8	41	32
1962/63	2	40	31	4	2	44	33
1963/64	2	9	5	3	3	12	8
Total		**218**	**125**	**20**	**16**	**238**	**141**

England: 6 caps (4 with Boro) 3 gls.

Peacock gives a display of the style that made him one of Boro's all-time top goalscorers.

In the 1961/62 season a Teesside businessman offered to buy a new overcoat for the first player to score a hat-trick. Alan Peacock claimed an early Christmas present with a three-goal performance against Norwich City at Carrow Road. There was however no win bonus to go with the coat. Boro lost 5-4.

Alan Peacock evades Boro colleague Mel Nurse (right) in an England v Wales international at Wembley.

"Although Brian Clough scored a lot of goals he was not a great leader of the line, Alan was. He showed for the ball in every position and was lethal in the air with his great heading ability. Alan was an all-round player."
Gordon Jones.

"Alan was a great support for Clough during their years together, though he really came into his own when Clough left becoming Boro's main goalscorer and he did even better at Leeds. He was very good in the air, worked hard and was overall a great player."
Dicky Rooks.

"The best player anyone could have had to work with. He got his fair share of goals but was unselfish and contributed a lot to my limited success in scoring goals. Off the field he was just the same as on it, unassuming. He got his just rewards in terms of England caps."
Brian Clough.

MY TOP 5
Alan Peacock

1. Wilf Mannion
2. Brian Clough
3. Alex McCrae
4. Bill Harris
5. George Hardwick

"He was my mate and he played for England - you don't do that without being a decent player. He was a workhorse, good in the air and put himself about."
Mel Nurse.

"Alan had great heading ability and a tremendous work-rate."
Ray Yeoman.

"Alan was a good target man in that if you had the ball and wanted a way out, you knew you could knock it to him and he'd keep hold of it. He was always available and centre-halves always found him difficult."
Mick McNeil.

"In the first game I saw Alan play against Leyton Orient he scored a hat-trick, He was in the team when I first joined the club and I learned a great deal from him. He had exceptional heading ability and he always had a lot of time for the young players."
Arthur Horsfield.

Stuart BOAM

" He was a rock at centre-half "

Born: Kirkby-in-Ashfield 28-01-48

A centre-half in every traditional sense, Stuart Boam captained Boro throughout one of the club's most successful decades - the 1970's.

Nottinghamshire-born Boam joined his local club Mansfield Town in 1966 and went on to make over 170 appearances for them up to May 1971.

Boro boss Stan Anderson snapped up the big defender for £50,000 and for the next eight years he was the rock on which the Boro defence was built.

Under Jack Charlton, Boam skippered Boro to the Second Division title in 1974, with the defence being the cornerstone of the side. He developed a formidable partnership with fellow central defender Willie Maddren and though he never received as much media acclaim as his colleague he was still treasured by Boro fans. Indeed a favourite chant of the Ayresome Park's Holgate End during his time at the club was: "Six foot two, eyes of blue, Stuart Boam is after you!" Boam and Maddren were the perfect foil for one another as the side successfully adapted to life in Division One. Between them they had every attribute that was required to cope with everything a top level strike force could throw at a defence.

It is still considered a great disappointment that Boam did not become the first Boro skipper to lift a major honour. The man who put his heart and soul into the club, and played in a side which threatened to lift silverware, only followed his Second Division success with the Anglo-Scottish Cup in 1975 - sadly a poor return for such a great leader.

On Charlton's departure, Boam had a run-in with new incumbent John Neal which resulted in him relinquishing the captaincy for a short period. However, Neal soon realised that Boam was the leader in the dressing room and restored him to the role of skipper.

However, on the eve of the 1979/80 season Boam left the club in a shock move to local Second Division rivals Newcastle for a fee of £100,000 - an excellent return on the £50,000 Anderson had paid considering he was now 31 and had given such loyal service to the club.

At St. James' Park, Boam made 69 appearances before returning to Mansfield as player-boss. He had further spells as a player with Hartlepool United and non-league Guisborough Town before once again returning to the Mansfield area, where he still lives.

Stuart Boam was a fine skipper in his time with Boro.

BORO RECORD 1971-79

Season	Div	League		Cup		Total	
		App	Gls	App	Gls	App	Gls
1971-72	2	38	0	8	0	46	0
1972-73	2	40	2	5	0	45	2
1973-74	2	42	4	5	0	47	4
1974-75	1	42	1	14	0	56	1
1975-76	1	39	3	17	1	56	4
1976-77	1	42	1	9	0	51	1
1977-78	1	39	2	9	1	48	3
1978-79	1	40	1	4	0	44	1
TOTAL		**322**	**14**	**71**	**2**	**393**	**16**

Stuart Boam

Boam shakes hands with Fulham skipper Alan Mullery before the first leg of the 1975 Anglo-Scottish Cup at Ayresome Park. Boro won the game 1-0 and took the trophy after a goal-less draw at Craven Cottage. The trophy is pictured on the right.

"Stuart was a collosus. He could tackle, he was an organiser and was great in the air. He was key to Boro winning promotion to the First Division under Jack Charlton."
Chris Kamara.

"He was a great captain. He really made sure that the youngsters who were in the squad were looked after and made to feel part of the squad but also kept the older lads happy. He was a great leader, keeping the squad together."
David Armstrong.

MY TOP 5
Stuart Boam

1. Graeme Souness
2. Bobby Murdoch
3. Willie Maddren
4. David Armstrong
5. John Hickton

"His attitude was excellent and the crowd loved him. Stuart was a winner. I remember in my big year watching from the Holgate that the crowd used to sing: "Six foot two, eyes of blue, Stuart Boam is after you'!

"He was so solid and stuck his foot in where it hurts. He was a good organiser and strong in the air. He was well respected by everybody he played with."
Mike Angus.

"He was a rock playing at centre-half and also scored important goals."
Bobby Murdoch.

"When I signed Stuart from Mansfield, he had a lot of raw edges. At Middlesbrough he became a top class defender. He was a very commanding centre-back. When I went to Mansfield to see him play I was also keen to sign his defensive partner but, at the time, we couldn't afford both so I went for Stuart. He was a great lad with lots of enthusiasm for the game and he allowed other players to play better giving them more space while he kept it tight at the back."
Stan Anderson.

Two of Boro's Best: Boam (right) with fellow 70's defender John Craggs before the last ever match at Ayresome Park in April 1995.

Dicky ROBINSON

" A great defender - quick and intelligent "

Born: Whitburn 19-02-27

When Boro signed the teenage Richard "Dicky" Robinson, he was seen as a potential star forward. But it was in defence that he was to make his name as one of the club's best ever players. As it turned out, Robinson did play one game as an emergency centre-forward for the club, in a 1-0 defeat at Manchester United in 1951, but he played the vast majority of his games at right-back or centre-half, though he showed his versatility with the occasional appearance at left-back.

After working down the mines as a Bevin Boy near Dunfermline during the war, 18-year-old Robinson joined Boro in April 1945 and was full-back partner to George Hardwick in the club's first league game when peace returned, a 1-0 win at Aston Villa. Over the next 13 years, he played over 400 games for the club, earning a reputation as a hard but classy full-back in a very good First Division Boro team. Although he never won an England cap, due to the consistency of Arsenal's Laurence Scott and later Spurs' Alf Ramsey, his stylish displays saw him represent the Football League five times between 1947 and 1951 in games against Irish and Scottish select sides. He also toured South Africa with a squad representing the FA.

A run of niggling injuries caused him to miss many games during the early 1950s and he struggled to rediscover his best form when he returned to the team. With the emergence of Ray Bilcliff, he was successfully switched to the centre of defence where he remained until accepting a move to Barrow in June 1959, aged 32. He had scored just one goal for Boro. After three seasons and another 139 league games for Barrow, he retired in 1962. He has remained in the North-west since ending his playing days.

Dicky Robinson was equally at home as a full-back or in the centre of defence - and, on one occasion, as an emergency centre-forward.

BORO RECORD 1946-59

Season	Div	League App	Gls	Cup App	Gls	Total App	Gls
1945/46	-	0	0	7	0	7	0
1946/47	1	40	0	7	0	47	0
1947/48	1	35	0	3	0	38	0
1948/49	1	41	0	1	0	42	0
1949/50	1	28	0	0	0	28	0
1950/51	1	33	0	1	0	34	0
1951/52	1	20	0	0	0	20	0
1952/53	1	24	0	0	0	24	0
1953/54	1	30	0	2	0	32	0
1954/55	2	33	0	0	0	33	0
1955/56	2	30	0	2	0	32	0
1956/57	2	39	1	3	0	42	1
1957/58	2	23	0	0	0	23	0
1958/59	2	14	0	0	0	14	0
TOTAL		**390**	**1**	**26**	**0**	**416**	**1**

Robinson in training at Ayresome Park during his Boro hey-day.

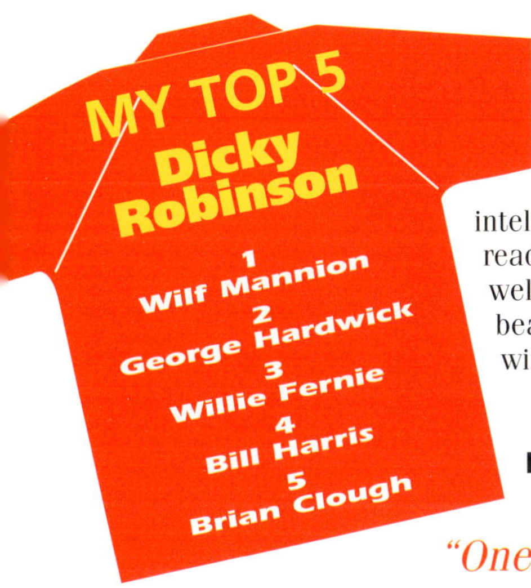

"Dicky was a great defender - pretty quick and very intelligent. He could read the game so well. He was rarely beaten by a winger."

Ray Billcliff.

I didn't see too much of Dicky but what I did see was his aggression and also the fact that he was two-footed and could ping the ball any distance."
Billy Horner.

"He was very important to the team and an excellent positional player. He was very fast, good in the air and could retrieve if he ever got beaten."
Harry Bell.

""He was the fastest full-back I've ever seen. He was a very strong defender and a great header of the ball."
Rolando Ugolini.

"One of the best all-round players I played with. He had two good feet, was good in the air and quick."
Ronnie Dicks.

Gary HAMILTON

" A great battler and a good footballer "

Born: Glasgow 27-12-65

Gary Hamilton's professional career was cruelly shortened by a knee injury but the battling Scot crammed in more than 200 appearances before being forced to give up the game in his mid-20s.

Hamilton first came to Boro for a one day trial after being recommended by the club's Scottish scout. He was invited back for a lengthier trial period and the young Glaswegian was signed up as an apprentice in January 1982.

The 17-year-old was given his debut by Malcolm Allison away to Bolton in February 1983 whilst still an apprentice and three months later signed on as a professional. Hamilton was still a teenager when he earned a regular slot in the Boro side as Willie Maddren and then Bruce Rioch managed the side, each making use of his whole hearted approach to the game.

Like most things in Hamilton's career, national recognition came early in the shape of Scotland Youth caps.

In the dark days of 1986, Hamilton was placed on the transfer list and when Boro slipped into the Third Division, Charlton offered him the chance to move south. But he remained loyal to the club and decided to ride out the club's troubles.

Hamilton had his one stint in the top flight after helping secure promotion through the play-offs in 1988. But throughout the season, as Boro battled against relegation, Hamilton was crippled with injury. And the visit to Sheffield Wednesday on May 13th 1989 which saw Boro go down, also proved to be Hamilton's last game for the club. He was only 24 but was never able to return to the Boro line-up.

After several failed come-backs from his knee injury, Hamilton was loaned out to Darlington in September 1991 but after just a handful of games, he was forced to retire. The great occasion of Boro's League Cup semi-final against Manchester United in March 1992 was tainted by the announcement at the game that Hamilton had made his decision to give up the game. He was awarded a testimonial against Sunderland in the 1993/94 season and is currently working as a coach in Texas.

Injury denied Gary Hamilton the chance to fulfil his potential but he became a favourite among fans and players.

BORO RECORD 1982-89

Season	Div	League App	Gls	Cup App	Gls	Total App	Gls
1982/83	2	8(1)	2	0	0	8(1)	2
1983/84	2	26(5)	3	3	0	29(5)	3
1984/85	2	34(2)	0	4	0	38(2)	0
1985/86	2	33	4	4	0	37	4
1986/87	3	41(2)	7	10(1)	3	51(3)	10
1987/88	2	40(1)	6	14	1	54(1)	7
1988/89	1	35(1)	3	7	0	42(1)	3
Total		**219(12)**	**25**	**42(1)**	**3**	**259(13)**	**29**

Hamilton (standing centre) celebrates with his Boro team-mates after the promotion play-off success over Chelsea in May 1988.

MY TOP 5
Jamie Pollock

1. Gary Hamilton
2. Stephen Pears
3. Tony Mowbray
4. Robbie Mustoe
5. Juninho

"He was an unsung hero - a great battler and a good footballer. He always gave as good as he got and never moaned about it."
Dean Glover.

"Hammy played for only a relatively short period but people did appreciate what he did. It's easy when things are hunky-dory, most players can play well then, but when the chips were down we always looked to Hammy to dig us out."
Stuart Ripley.

Hamilton rifles in a spectacular goal against Fulham.

"He had great battling qualities and stuck with the club through the disappointing times. He was a superb professional."
Jamie Pollock.

"He was a battler with the will to win. He was good to have in the team because he never gave up. When he got injured he tried everything he could, just like when he played, to get back and that summed him up."
Nicky Mohan.

MY TOP 5
Gary Hamilton

1. Stephen Pears
2. Heine Otto
3. Bernie Slaven
4. Tony Mowbray
5. Juninho

George CAMSELL

" A phenomenal goalscorer for club and country "

Born: Framwellgate Moor, County Durham 27-11-02

The incredible feat of 59 league goals in 37 games will forever stand as testimony to George Camsell's ability in front of goal. The Boro record from the 1926/27 season is never likely to be eclipsed but Camsell was no one season wonder and even translated his devastating form to the international stage. Only the presence of Everton's Dixie Dean at the summit of the 'most goals in a season' table with one extra goal from two more games, and a strange lack of faith from the England selectors, robbed Camsell of his rightful place among the all-time greats.

Camsell signed for Boro from Third Division North side Durham City for £600 in October 1925. He started his Boro career as an outside-left to little effect and had Barnsley been able to afford a £200 fee, his amazing achievements would never have occurred, with Boro.

The 1926/27 season initially showed little indication of what was to follow when, after a disastrous start of three defeats and a draw, Camsell stepped into the centre-forward position for the visit of Hull to Ayresome Park. It brought the first victory and when Camsell's name appeared twice on the scoresheet in the following game it started the incredible run that was to bring 59 goals in 37 league games - 63 goals in 40 games in all competitions - as Boro raced clear at the top of the Second Division. The season included 10 hat-tricks from the brave centre-forward including all five in a 5-3 win over Manchester City.

The next season saw Camsell continue to impress but incredibly, despite his 33 goals, Boro were relegated from the First Division. More goals came as Boro bounced back at the first attempt and his scoring form was crucial in cementing the club in the top flight averaging easily more than a goal every two games in all but one of the next 10 seasons.

England recognition was only a matter of time and the first cap came against France in May 1929. It seems incredible that Camsell was capped only nine times for his country, especially when those nine games brought 18 goals. After a hat-trick against Wales in November 1929, and 11 goals in four games, Camsell was bizarrely left out of the team for the next four years and even when recalled, despite scoring every time he played, never reached double figures in terms of caps.

The war marked the end of Camsell's Boro career but he served the club as chief scout, coach and assistant secretary in a further two decades with the club. He died in Middlesbrough in 1966.

Boro's all-time top scorer: George Camsell.

BORO RECORD 1925-39

Season	Div	League App	League Gls	Cup App	Cup Gls	Total App	Total Gls
1925/26	2	4	3	0	0	4	3
1926/27	2	37	59	3	4	40	63
1927/28	1	40	33	3	4	43	36
1928/29	2	40	30	3	3	43	33
1929/30	1	34	29	4	2	38	31
1930/31	1	37	32	2	0	39	32
1931/32	1	37	20	2	0	39	20
1932/33	1	31	17	4	1	35	18
1933/34	1	36	23	2	1	38	24
1934/35	1	26	14	2	0	28	14
1935/36	1	38	28	4	4	42	32
1936/37	1	23	18	1	0	24	18
1937/38	1	24	9	3	1	27	10
1938/39	1	11	10	2	0	13	10
Total		**418**	**325**	**35**	**20**	**453**	**345**

England: 9 caps (all with Boro) 18 gls.

MY TOP 5
Ralph Birkett

1. Wilf Mannion
2. George Hardwick
3. Bob Baxter
4. Dave Cumming
5. George Camsell

A rare shot of Camsell with the ball at his feet. With George around, it was usually in the back of the net!

"To have scored as many goals as he did for Middlesbrough, you had to be a brilliant centre-forward. He was very brave and would shoot from anywhere."
Ralph Birkett.

"George was a noted goalscorer. He was a brilliant player and scored a lot when he got his England caps. He was also very strong and hard to get off the ball."
Micky Fenton.

"George was a phenomenal goalscorer for club and country. His record will never be beaten."
Bill Gates.

Boro signed George Camsell from Durham City in 1925 after failing to convince Tranmere to sell their young striker Dixie Dean.

MY TOP 5
Bill Gates

1. Wilf Mannion
2. George Camsell
3. Brian Clough
4. Graeme Souness
5. John Hickton

Stuart RIPLEY

" Could put the fear of death into any defender "

Born: Middlesbrough 20-11-67

Speedy, rampaging winger Stuart Ripley progressed through from Boro Boys to become a crucial element in three promotions and only the third Boro player to break the £1 million transfer barrier. Despite making an exceptional number of his Boro appearances as a substitute, Ripley was a vital creative ingredient in the Boro side for eight seasons.

Ripley's first taste of league football came as a Boro substitute for Irving Nattrass against Oldham in February 1985. A year later, he was allowed to join Third Division Bolton on loan. He scored his first league goal on his debut for the Trotters. On his return to Ayresome Park, Ripley did not have to wait long for another chance, coming in for a run of eight games at the end of the season. But it was on a trip to China with the England Youth team that he heard of Boro's relegation to the Third Division.

Ripley was the regular number 11 as Boro bounced back at the first attempt and scored his first hat-trick - and six vital goals in as many games - in the lead-up to the play-offs that led Boro into the top flight in 1988. The first of seven England under-21 caps came against Russia that summer when Ripley appeared along with Boro team-mate Colin Cooper in the Toulon tournament.

When Boro were relegated at the end of the 1988/89 season, Ripley was expected to leave but stayed loyal to the club. Despite being used as a frequent substitute for the next two seasons by Bruce Rioch and then Colin Todd, he was a regular thorn in in the side of opposition defences and when Boro secured promotion in 1992, Kenny Dalglish paid out £1.3 million to take him to Ewood Park.

Injury has disrupted Ripley's career since the move to Lancashire but his form was crucial in securing the Premier League title in 1995. His solitary England cap came courtesy of Graham Taylor, who selected the winger for his last game as England manager in San Marino in 1994.

Stuart Ripley in action during a pre-season friendly in 1989.

BORO RECORD 1984-92

Season	Div	League App	Gls	Cup App	Gls	Total App	Gls
1984/85	2	0(1)	0	0	0	0(1)	0
1985/86	2	7(1)	0	1	0	8(1)	0
1986/87	3	43(1)	4	11(1)	3	54(2)	7
1987/88	2	40(3)	8	13	1	53(3)	9
1988/89	1	36	4	6	0	42	4
1989/90	2	26(13)	1	10	0	36(13)	1
1990/91	2	22(17)	6	6(3)	1	28(20)	7
1991/92	2	36(3)	3	12	1	48(3)	4
Total		**210(39)**	**26**	**59(4)**	**6**	**269(43)**	**32**

England: 1 cap (none with Boro) 0 gls

A Notts County defender is grounded as Ripley tears towards the goal-mouth in this 1-0 home win in September 1990.

"You could give the ball to Stuart and he would run down the line and take the pressure off the back four. He was a good crosser and has done very well for himself."
Stephen Pears.

"A local lad who done good. Ripper was like lightning and he put the fear of death into any defender who was marking him. Without doubt, Ripper created a lot of space for me with his many runs forward while he was also a great provider."
Bernie Slaven.

MY TOP 5
Stuart Ripley

1. Tony Mowbray
2. Bernie Slaven
3. Gary Pallister
4. Gary Hamilton
5. Craig Johnston

"On his day he was unstoppable. I remember playing against Portsmouth and he was up against John Beresford and ran him ragged for 90 minutes. He's a two-footed player who scores goals as well as creating them."
Jimmy Phillips.

"He had pace, was strong and direct and had a powerful shot as well."
Trevor Senior.

"He's a good crosser, works hard and has done very well. He always likes a good laugh as well."
Trevor Putney.

"Stuart was a quality wide player, quick, direct and a good crosser of the ball.
He always did well for the team and Kenny Dalglish must have thought a lot of him because he paid £1 million to get him."
Robbie Mustoe.

Alex McCRAE

" An inside-forward with a lot of flair who could score goals "

Born: Stoneyburn 02-01-20

Alex McCrae can count himself unfortunate to have played for Middlesbrough at the same time as the legendary Wilf Mannion. For in any other era, his skills would surely have ensured his place in the club's hall of fame.

McCrae's best season for the club was 1950/51 when he netted 21 league goals from inside-forward, all but one of them before Christmas. A run of 20 goals in just 24 games catapulted Boro into a race for the First Division championship but when injury and loss of form caused the goals to dry up for McCrae, the title challenge evaporated.

McCrae began his professional career with Hearts in 1941, moving into English football six years later with Charlton Athletic. However, just 43 league games and eight goals later, he joined Boro for £10,000 in October 1948 after turning down a move to Sheffield United. Although he initially struggled to find his best form, left-footer McCrae became a firm favourite at Ayresome Park and struck the winner in a 1-0 derby victory over North-east rivals Newcastle United at St James' Park on Boxing Day 1949. He ended the campaign as 16-goal top scorer.

His pace and fine shot brought him a hatful of goals the following season but he left the club in March 1953 when he joined Falkirk. He went on to coach Ballymena United in Northern Ireland before returning to Scottish football for a two-month spell as manager of Stirling Albion. After another period with Falkirk, he was appointed as Boro's scout in Scotland in 1966. He currently lives in West Lothian.

McCrae (centre) in training with Jimmy Gordon (left) and Lindy Delapenha at a snowy Ayresome Park.

BORO RECORD 1948-53

Season	Div	League App	Gls	Cup App	Gls	Total App	Gls
1948/49	1	20	2	0	0	20	2
1949/50	1	36	14	4	2	40	16
1950/51	1	32	21	1	0	33	21
1951/52	1	24	6	2	0	26	6
1952/53	1	10	4	1	0	11	4
Total		**122**	**47**	**8**	**2**	**130**	**49**

Alex McCrae (centre) was a versatile member of Boro's post-war side, here in training with left to right Wilf Mannion, Harry Bell, Rolando Ugolini and George Hardwick.

"I idolised him as a kid. He was an inside-forward with a lot of flair who could score goals. I used to watch him and go home thinking I wanted to be like him."
Alan Peacock.

"Alex was a great player and one hell of a nice man who scored a lot of goals in a very exciting side."
George Hardwick.

"He was a brilliant player, very good positionally. He was a pleasant lad who was a real family man and a pleasure to play alongside. With him and little Wilfie I was always well supported. I was lucky to be in such a good side."
Johnny Spuhler.

MY TOP 5
Alex McCrae

1. Wilf Mannion
2. George Hardwick
3. Bob Baxter
4. Jimmy Gordon
5. Rolando Ugolini

Terry COOPER

" He was the classic left wing-back "

Born: Castleford 12-07-44

Terry Cooper's celebrated England days were behind him when he joined Boro in 1975. But former Leeds team-mate Jack Charlton's decision to bring the 31-year-old to Ayresome Park paid off when Cooper's fine attacking play from left-back played a crucial part in establishing the club in the First Divison.

Cooper had joined Leeds as a 16-year-old, progressing through the ranks and switching from left-wing to left-back. Don Revie prompted the change of position and gave Cooper his debut in the 1963/64 season. Cooper stood firm at left-back through Leeds' most successful period. He helped the club to two league titles and two Fairs Cup triumphs. He also scored the winner in the club's League Cup success of 1967.

The first of 20 England caps came against France at Wembley in 1969 and Cooper was one of his country's stars of the 1970 World Cup in Mexico before eventually losing his place to Emlyn Hughes.

Jack Charlton paid £50,000 to take Cooper to Ayresome Park and his classy performances on the left flank proved a good asset to the club's revival. He made his debut against Spurs in March 1975, displacing Frank Spraggon at left-back. He scored his only Boro goal in a victory over Liverpool a year later. But Cooper's Boro career came to an unsavoury conclusion when he refused to go on a tour to Norway and was suspended by the club. He requested a transfer and linked up with another former Leeds colleague, Norman Hunter, at Bristol City.

Player-manager spells followed at Bristol Rovers, Doncaster - alongside yet another Leeds old boy Billy Bremner - and back at Bristol City before hanging up his boots, aged 40, in 1984. He helped the Ashton Gate club to two Wembley finals in the Freight Rover Trophy and became Britain's first player-director before moving on to Exeter City for two spells as manager, interspersed with two years at Birmingham. He is currently first team coach alongside Graeme Souness at Southampton.

Terry Cooper - with that unmistakeable moustache - was a true bargain signing by Jack Charlton.

BORO RECORD 1974/78

Season	Div	League App	Gls	Cup App	Gls	Total App	Gls
1974/75	1	9	0	0	0	9	0
1975/76	1	40	1	15	0	55	1
1976/77	1	40	0	9	0	49	0
1977/78	1	16	0	4	0	20	0
Total		**105**	**1**	**28**	**0**	**133**	**1**

England: 20 caps (none with Boro) 0 gls.

Former England full-back Cooper in training for Boro.

MY TOP 5
Terry Cooper

1. Graeme Souness
2. Willie Maddren
3. John Hickton
4. Bobby Murdoch
5. Juninho

"Terry played in my position - left-back. He was great at taking people on and he never lost the ball. He could go down either wing or cut inside, making angles for other players. A great crosser of the ball."
Peter Johnson.

"Terry was a member of the England squad from the 1970 World Cup but he still had all the skill when he moved to Boro. He was a very skilful player and he passed on his experience to all the younger players."
Graeme Hedley.

"He would have played for England even now because he was the classic left wing-back. He had the intricacies of a skilful winger and the tenacity of a ball-winning full-back He really was that good. He was approaching the end of his career at Middlesbrough but he was still exceptionally good."
Alf Wood.

Rolando UGOLINI

"A good goalkeeper and a real character"

Born: Lucca 04-06-24

Many years before Ravanelli and Festa, Boro's first Italian connection came in the shape of athletic goalkeeper Rolando Ugolini. The Italian-born number one is remembered as one of the club's best ever goalkeepers from his eight-year post-war spell.

Ugolini, in fact, grew up in Scotland. He moved to Glasgow aged one and became a naturalised Scot. His career started at Hearts before a period at Celtic as reserve to Scottish international Willie Miller. After turning down a move to Chelsea, Ugolini finally agreed to move south of the border to join Boro for £7,000 in May 1948.

His first game - a seven goal defeat in a practice game - was an inauspicious start but "Ugo" quickly established himself as a popular number one with the club's players and fans, replacing Derek Goodfellow as goalkeeper from the start of the 1948/49 season when he made his debut against Chelsea. He was renowned as an eccentric dressing room character and was nicknamed "Rolando the Cat".

Over the next nine years, Ugolini was the regular keeper, helping the club stay in the First Division until relegation came in 1954. The highlight was a sixth place in Division One in 1951.

By the end of the 1955/56 season, Ugolini had been displaced by Peter Taylor and after spending the following campaign as second choice left Boro to join Third Division Wrexham. After two years, he returned to Scotland for a spell with Dundee United before retiring. He ran several betting shops and lives in Scotland today.

Back at Ayresome: Rolando Ugolini walks on to the pitch for a hero's welcome in February 1995 when he returned to Teesside from his home in Scotland to celebrate George Hardwick's birthday.

BORO RECORD 1948-56

Season	Div	League App	Gls	Cup App	Gls	Total App	Gls
1948/49	1	39	0	1	0	40	0
1949/50	1	41	0	4	0	45	0
1950/51	1	42	0	1	0	43	0
1951/52	1	41	0	3	0	44	0
1952/53	1	41	0	1	0	42	0
1953/54	1	42	0	2	0	44	0
1954/55	2	38	0	1	0	39	0
1955/56	2	36	0	2	0	38	0
Total		**320**	**0**	**15**	**0**	**335**	**0**

A dramatic dive from Ugolini in a Wear-Tees derby at Roker Park.

"The sort of character that every club needs. Apart from being a good goalkeeper, he was the bubbly one. In training, we used to do one-and-a-half hours running and ten minutes with the football and then at 12.30 we were out on a limb. After we had a milkshake at Rea's cafe, Rolando used to organise the afternoon sessions. He organised head tennis and we played for two bob. He was brilliant at it. The approach he had to football is essential to any side. Football does get you down on occasions but he was a bubbly character. I met him a couple of years ago and he was just the same. After I saw him, I spent all my time reminiscing about him."

Brian Clough.

MY TOP 5
Rolando Ugolini

1. Wilf Mannion
2. George Hardwick
3. Lindy Delapenha
4. Brian Clough
5. Dicky Robinson

"Rolando was from the era when I watched the Boro. He was a great bloke who was agile and athletic. He was also a bit of a showman while very commanding. If a forward ran into Rolando he was dead!"
Billy Day.

"Rolando was a real character who was always a very happy person to have around the dressing room."
George Hardwick.

"He was probably the best goalkeeper I saw at Boro."
Geoff Walker.

"A good goalkeeper and he kept the dressing room going."
Alex McCrae.

MY TOP 5
Billy Day

1. Rolando Ugolini
2. Wilf Mannion
3. George Hardwick
4. Brian Clough
5. Bill Harris

Jim PLATT

" You always felt secure with Jim in goal "

Born: Ballymoney 26-01-52

A Boro career that was to span more than a decade, and see arguably the best ever Boro side, began when Stan Anderson paid £7,000 for the 18-year-old Jim Platt. The young Irishman had impressed playing for Ballymena and, before joining Boro, had interested Liverpool. Platt had a three-week trial at Anfield but the signing of Ray Clemence scuppered any deal and Liverpool's loss proved to be Boro's gain.

After a homesick season on the sidelines, Platt took over the number one shirt from Willie Whigham two months into the 1971/72 season. After two successive defeats in which seven goals had been conceded, Anderson brought in the young debutant and two clean sheets followed. Platt's form earned him the club's player of the year award at the end of the season.

The following season Platt was ever-present and he played a crucial role as Boro stormed to the Second Division title in 1973/74, conceding just 28 goals in 40 games, including an impressive 23 clean sheets. Platt kept a regular place between the sticks in the First Division, only occasionally making way for Pat Cuff.

By the 1977/78 season, competition for places with Cuff and David Brown restricted Platt's appearances and the arrival of Jim Stewart for the start of the 1978/79 campaign meant a time out of the side. But after spells on loan at Hartlepool and Cardiff, Platt bounced back to reclaim the number one shirt for the second half of the season and it was not until the middle of the 1982/83 season that he once again lost his place. Kelham O'Hanlon was brought in by new manager Malcolm Allison while Platt was injured and Platt, as with many senior players at the time, soon left the club.

His sterling performances for Boro brought him recognition for Northern Ireland. He earned 23 caps and it was only the presence of Pat Jennings that restricted his appearances. Platt made his debut for Northern Ireland in 1976 as a substitute against Israel, and went on to feature in his country's strongest period and played one game in the 1982 World Cup Finals.

After leaving Boro, Platt returned to Northern Ireland and Ballymena where he was player-manager. After working with several clubs and running his own printing and wholesaling business, he returned to the North-East as assistant to former Boro team-mate David Hodgson at Darlington. When Hodgson left, Platt took over at the helm but was dismissed early in the 1996/97 season. He took over as manager of Gateshead in January 1997.

Jim Platt has returned to the North-east in recent years to manage Darlington and Gateshead.

BORO RECORD 1971-83

Season	Div	League App	League Gls	Cup App	Cup Gls	Total App	Total Gls
1971/72	2	33	0	6	0	39	0
1972/73	2	42	0	5	0	47	0
1973/74	2	40	0	5	0	45	0
1974/75	1	42	0	14	0	56	0
1975/76	1	41	0	16	0	57	0
1976/77	1	24	0	3	0	27	0
1977/78	1	22	0	9	0	31	0
1978/79	1	15	0	0	0	15	0
1979/80	1	37	0	6	0	43	0
1980/81	1	40	0	7	0	47	0
1981/82	1	42	0	5	0	47	0
1982/83	2	23	0	4	0	27	0
Total		**401**	**0**	**80**	**0**	**481**	**0**

Northern Ireland: 23 caps (20 with Boro) 0 gls.

MY TOP 5
Jim Platt

1 Graeme Souness
2 Willie Maddren
3 David Armstrong
4 John Hickton
5 Bobby Murdoch

"When I was a kid at the club, Jim always had time for us young lads and a nice word to say. Every time I have seen him he always takes time for you. He is a genuine bloke. He also represented his country and was the goalkeeper in one of the best ever Boro sides under Jack Charlton."
Colin Cooper.

"You always felt secure with Jim in goal. He never panicked and always dominated the box. He was a very confident player who always gave confidence to the rest of the team."
John Hickton.

"He was the elder statesman when I came to the club as an apprentice but he was a great character to be around and always quick with advice for us younger lads."
Alan Kernaghan.

Sporting the shirts of sponsors McLean Homes are Jim Platt and team-mates Darren Wood (left) and Mick Kennedy.

Ian GIBSON

" A gifted player but a wasted talent "

Born: Newton Stewart 30-03-43

Young Scotsman Ian Gibson was hailed as "the new Wilf Mannion" when Bob Dennison brought him to Middlesbrough in March 1962. In his four years with the club he showed he was one of the most naturally talented players to have turned out for Boro but a career that promised so much, failed to reach the potential heights many anticipated.

As a youngster, Gibson had played for Scotland Schoolboys and was offered the chance of joining Rangers. But on the advice of his father, Gibson waited for an opportunity to come to England and it was Fourth Division Accrington Stanley that gave him his chance. Gibson became one of the youngest ever to have played in the League when he appeared for the Accies aged just 15. He was registered as an amateur at the club and Gibson opted to move to Bradford Park Avenue after a year at Accrington, to sign professional forms. Accrington protested at the move and the Football League called a special meeting before allowing it to go through. The promising midfielder helped his new side win promotion into the Third Division before moving north to Ayresome Park.

Bob Dennison intended to carefully nurture his new prodigy but injuries to Taffy Orritt and Alan Peacock forced the manager's hand and 18-year-old Gibson made his Boro debut on a trip to Scunthorpe in March 1962. He notched his first goal in his next start and scored twice as Boro trounced Bristol Rovers 5-0 at Ayresome Park in April. Dennison kept faith with the young star and he was a regular, on the scoresheet as well as the teamsheet over the coming seasons. He was picked twice for Scotland's under-23 side in the 1963/64 season.

Boro manager Raich Carter handed Gibson the captaincy for the 1965/66 campaign, making him the club's youngest ever skipper at the age of 22, but Boro slid down the table and relegation to the Third Division followed. The drop was too much for the ambitious Scot who was keen to play at the top level and Second Division Coventry City swooped. Sky Blues manager Jimmy Hill persuaded his board to part with £57,500 - then a record sale for Boro.

Just three months after the move to Highfield Road, Gibson fell out with Hill and asked for a transfer. But when the side looked out of the promotion chase mid-season, Gibson was reinstated, scoring twice on his return and helping the team to an unbeaten run that led to promotion. The remaining four seasons at Coventry were hindered by injury and disputes with the management and Gibson moved on to Cardiff in 1970 before ending his career at Bournemouth. He managed just 20 games for the Cherries before an Achilles heel injury forced him into retirement. He later returned to Teesside where he lives today.

Unlucky to have played for Boro during one of the club's more unsuccessful periods, Ian Gibson still made his mark at Ayresome Park.

BORO RECORD 1961-66

Season	Div	League App	Gls	Cup App	Gls	Total App	Gls
1961/62	2	8	3	0	0	8	3
1962/63	2	39	12	5	1	44	13
1963/64	2	42	14	3	0	45	14
1964/65	2	41	8	4	1	45	9
1965/66	2	38	7	4	1	42	8
Total		**168**	**44**	**16**	**3**	**184**	**47**

" He went on to Coventry while I was at the club but he was a young lad of about 20 when I joined and I didn't realise the potential he had. He was good on the ball and had a great touch. There was something special about him."
Mel Nurse.

"Ian was a superb player, a different class. I used to watch him at first, then I ended up playing a few games with him. He had great vision, was very inventive and he was always there to pick up the pieces. He was a very strong player."
Geoff Butler.

"I was already at the club when Ian Gibson arrived and he was a very talented player. Unfortunately, he became a wasted talent. If a club could have got him by the scruff of the neck like they do now, he could have gone on to win 100 caps for Scotland."
Arthur Horsfield.

MY TOP 5
Geoff Butler

1. Brian Clough
2. Ian Gibson
3. Graeme Souness
4. Wilf Mannion
5. George Hardwick

"He was a very talented midfielder with a good all-round game and could score goals. He could also win you matches out of nothing."
Billy Horner.

Class of 1963. Ian Gibson (front row, second from the left) lines up with his team-mates. Other members of Boro's Best are: Alan Peacock (front centre) Bill Harris (front second right) and Mick McNeil (second row, second left).

David HODGSON

" Everything a supporter wants in a player "

Born: Gateshead 01-11-60

Boro fans will long remember young striker David Hodgson for his lightning pace and special rapport with those who stood on the Holgate End at Ayresome Park. When he wasn't on the field making his direct runs, setting up more chances than he put away, Hodgson was known to stand on the Holgate with the supporters cheering on his team-mates.

Hodgson joined Boro on his 16th birthday after trial spells with Ipswich, Bolton and Sheffield Wednesday, progressing into the first team in time for a debut in September 1978. After tasting the action twice as a substitute, Hodgson made his first start in a home game against Bristol City in November. And his first goal came when reverting to a substitute for his next game two months later.

Over the following seasons, Hodgson's contribution came mostly in the shape of assists for others. His goalscoring record was his main let-down but he netted a hat-trick in December 1980 in a 4-1 victory over Spurs. England under-21 caps came with a debut against Norway at the Dell in September 1980. Hodgson partnered Craig Johnston in two of his six under-21 games while with Boro and the club had the unprecedented honour of three players being selected when Mark Proctor joined the pair in a match against Ireland at Anfield in 1981.

But when Boro were relegated at the end of the 1981/82 season, Hodgson followed in the footsteps of Johnston and Graeme Souness by making a £450,000 switch to Liverpool. Unlike his two predecessors, however, Hodgson was not a success at Anfield and his subsequent career was one of disappointment. After 28 league games for Liverpool, Hodgson was sold to Sunderland for £125,000 where he played in the 1985 League Cup final against his next club, Norwich.

In early 1987, Hodgson returned to Boro for a loan spell but the move ended in disaster when he was sent off in his second game and returned to Carrow Road. The later days of Hodgson's career proved nomadic and saw him turn out for Swansea and Sheffield Wednesday as well as spells with Metz in France, Mazda in Japan and Spanish club Jerez. After a spell as a football agent then moved into management with Darlington where he is currently in a second spell in charge.

David Hodgson stood on the Holgate with the fans when he could not play for the club.

BORO RECORD 1978-82 & 86

Season	Div	League App	Gls	Cup App	Gls	Total App	Gls
1978/79	1	13(6)	1	0	0	13(6)	1
1979/80	1	40	7	6	1	46	8
1980/81	1	32	5	6	3	38	8
1981/82	1	31(3)	3	3	0	34(3)	3
1986/87	3	2	0	0	0	2	0
Total		**118(9)**	**16**	**15**	**4**	**133(9)**	**20**

Hodgy with another who might have made it into Boro's Best, a certain George Best, who is pictured in Boro colours for Jim Platt's testimonial match in 1981. Best agreed to join the club but failed to turn up to sign the deal.

"Hodgson had a tremendous attitude and worked very hard. He was a gem to work with. He learnt a lot from Bosco Jankovic when he started out and finished up a very good player. He was very raw at the start but he got better and better. He always looked forward to going out and scoring goals."
John Neal.

MY TOP 5
David Hodgson

1. Graeme Souness
2. David Armstrong
3. Bobby Murdoch
4. Mark Proctor
5. Bernie Slaven

"He never fulfilled his potential and Boro fans saw the best of him in the First Division. He had pace and was direct, he scored goals and was brave. An unselfish player up front, I thought he would go on to play for England but I think Liverpool was the wrong choice of club - he should have moved where there was not so much expectation."
Irving Nattrass.

"Hodgy typified everything a supporter wanted in a player. I was in senior school when he started playing for Boro and he was always my favourite, not just because of his playing ability. On one occasion, when he was suspended, he came and stood on the Holgate with the fans and I remember giving him my scarf. He was truly one of the lads. As a player, he wasn't a great goalscorer but he was dynamic and always gave 100 per cent commitment. He was my boyhood hero, the true king of Ayresome Park."
Lee Turnbull.

MY TOP 5
Lee Turnbull

1. David Hodgson
2. Bernie Slaven
3. Craig Johnston
4. Tony Mowbray
5. Terry Cochrane

"I liked him a lot. He was a big influence on me when I was at the club, he was all enthusiasm."
Darren Wood.

Mark PROCTOR

" An under-rated player and a great passer "

Born: Middlesbrough 30-01-61

Mark Proctor's eight seasons at Ayresome Park were separated by seven years away from Teesside but it was Middlesbrough that saw the best of the talented, homegrown midfielder.

As a youngster, Proctor was offered a trial by Leeds but homesickness brought him back to Teesside where he signed on as a schoolboy. While moving through the ranks, Proctor was called up into the England Youth set-up and captained his country at this level. John Neal was manager when Proctor turned professional in 1978 and Neal gave the youngster his debut on a visit to Birmingham in August of that year at the age of 17. His first of nine goals in a highly promising first season came in a 7-2 mauling of Chelsea at Ayresome Park.

England under-21 caps came in 1981, against Ireland and Switzerland, before the highly sought-after 20-year-old was signed by Nottingham Forest's Brian Clough for £440,000 in August 1981. More under-21 caps followed but 18 months and 60 games later, he was loaned out to Sunderland before moving permanently to Roker Park. More than 100 games followed for Sunderland but Boro's neighbours dropped out of the First Division in 1985 and when the Roker club started the 1987-88 season in the Third, Proctor moved to top flight Sheffield Wednesday for £275.000. And his career came full circle 18 months later when Proctor made a surprise return to Boro. The deadline day deal in 1989 cost Bruce Rioch £300,000.

His arrival came too late to save the club from relegation but Proctor helped Boro reach the play-offs in 1991 and finally secure promotion under Lennie Lawrence in 1993. But as Boro dropped out of the Premier League in the following season, Proctor started just six games and was given a loan spell at Tranmere where he renewed his acquaintance with the play-offs. When the season ended, Proctor was released by Boro and made the move to Tranmere permanent. After ending his career, Proctor returned to Teesside to work with the Football Academy and schoolboy sides at Middlesbrough.

He also appeared briefly for Blyth Spartans and made a surprise return to League football in March 1997 to help out struggling Hartlepool.

Mark Proctor pictured during his second spell as a Boro player.

BORO RECORD 1978-81 & 89-93

Season	Div	League App	Gls	Cup App	Gls	Total App	Gls
1978/79	1	31(2)	9	4	0	35(2)	9
1979/80	1	38	2	5	0	43	2
1980/81	1	38	1	7	2	45	3
1988/89	1	10	0	0	0	10	0
1989/90	2	45	4	12	0	57	4
1990/91	2	15(5)	0	2(1)	0	17(6)	0
1991/92	2	27(9)	2	6(4)	0	33(13)	2
1992/93	P	6(5)	0	0(1)	0	6(6)	0
Total		**210(21)**	**18**	**36(6)**	**2**	**246(27)**	**20**

"He was another player Boro saw the best of and he never fulfilled his potential. I was convinced he would go on to play for England in a Paul Ince or David Batty style role. He was the sort of player who could hold things together. A good player."
Irving Nattrass.

"He had great technical ability and was a good distributor of the ball. He scored a few goals as well."
Darren Wood.

"Mark was a very uncomplicated player and a great passer of the ball. An excellent link between defence and attack, he used to get and give it. He used to play within a very tight area."
Peter Johnson.

MY TOP 5
Mark Proctor

1. John Hickton
2. Graeme Souness
3. Stuart Boam
4. John O'Rourke
5. Bernie Slaven

"Whatever I achieved at Middlesbrough, he provided. He was a good pro to play alongside."
David Hodgson.

When Mark Proctor joined the Boro staff as a youngster, his tasks included cleaning the boots and running errands for his boyhood idol, Graeme Souness.

"I actually saw more of Proctor when he was at Sheffield Wednesday but I always liked him as a player. He was always very 'steady Eddie' and extremely under-rated. He always seemed to play well and rarely lost the ball. Teams need that type of player."
Neil Cox.

All smiles despite defeat as Proctor acknowledges the fantastic support of the Boro fans after the 1990 ZDS Cup final loss at Wembley.

Nick BARMBY

" A versatile and intelligent young player "

Born: Hull 11-02-74

When Nick Barmby joined Middlesbrough on the eve of the 1995/96 season he became the first current England international to join the club since Steve Bloomer 89 years earlier. His £5.25 million fee smashed the club's previous transfer record (held by Jan Fjortoft) four times over but manager Bryan Robson knew he was buying quality. Alas, it was to all end in tears with Barmby's transfer to Everton just 15 months later.

A star member of the England youth side, Barmby broke into the Tottenham first team as a teenager, displaying a fine football brain and a versatility that made him equally at home in midfield or in attack. He scored his first league goal during the 1992/93 campaign, ironically in a 2-2 draw with Middlesbrough, and went on to progress into the full England side by his 21st birthday. Clearly his natural ability was allowed to blossom under the watchful eye of successive Spurs managers, Terry Venables, Ossie Ardiles and Gerry Francis.

Keen to return to the north, Barmby jumped at the chance to link up with Bryan Robson and help Boro establish themselves on their return to the Premiership. He immediately hit top form on Teesside, playing a part in almost every goal the team scored as they soared to fourth place in the top flight. His deadly partnership with and similarity in appearance to Craig Hignett 'in the hole' behind striker Fjortoft earned the pair the title of 'The Midget Gems' and Barmby won more England caps under his former Spurs boss, Venables.

His form dipped on the arrival of Juninho and it seemed the club's stars were incompatible as their playing styles were so similar. Although he ended the season as the club's nine-goal top scorer, he did not hit the target in the final four months of the campaign as the whole team struggled for form. However, two goals in a friendly against China clinched his place in the England squad for Euro 96 and he made three substitute appearances during the tournament. Robson persevered with the Barmby-Juninho pairing into the 1996/97 campaign but, in need of cash to strengthen his defence, finally sold his England star to Everton for £5.75 million in October 1996.

Nick Barmby's time on Teesside was all too brief but he impressed with his intelligent play while wearing the Boro shirt. He's pictured on his goal-scoring debut at Arsenal.

BORO RECORD 1995/96

Season	Div	League App	Gls	Cup App	Gls	Total App	Gls
1995-96	P	32	7	7	2	39	9
1996-97	P	10	1	0	0	10	1
Total		**42**	**8**	**7**	**2**	**49**	**10**

England: 10 caps (8 with Boro) 3 gls.

"Nick was a young lad who arrived at Middlesbrough with a lot of pressure on him because of the big fee. People seemed to forget just how young he was but he was a terrific player. Nick made a great start and he handled the pressure superbly. A great player of one-two's and a very busy player who will make as many, if not more, than he scores."
Bernie Slaven.

"His all-round play was excellent. He's a very intelligent player with a first class attitude."
Craig Hignett.

Barmby's early form helped Boro climb the league at the start of the 1995/96 season including this win over Blackburn at the Cellnet Riverside Stadium when he scored.

MY TOP 5
Craig Hignett

1. Nick Barmby
2. Steve Pears
3. Emerson
4. Robbie Mustoe
5. Juninho

"Nick is a very good player who was under a lot of pressure after his big money transfer to Boro. It may not have worked out how everyone hoped but I'm sure he'll go on to become an England regular for many years. He always worked hard when he was at Boro and was very dangerous. He was also versatile in that he could play up front, behind the main strikers or in midfield."
Neil Cox.

Colin COOPER

"A stylish and reliable defender"

Born: Sedgefield 28-02-67

As a centre-back, Colin Cooper became a £1 million player and played for England but at Boro he was a respected left-back as the team won two successive promotions. The position is even more unlikely considering he was a naturally right-footed player but Cooper made the role his own and was a crucial member of Bruce Rioch's team.

Boro beat off competition from Newcastle and Crystal Palace to sign Cooper as a schoolboy and he progressed through the youth ranks at Ayresome Park to turn professional in the summer of 1984. A first-team league debut came as a substitute against Crystal Palace in March 1986, after earlier playing in a Full Members Cup tie at Hull, and by the start of the next campaign, Cooper, aged 19, had won a place at left-back.

Under the managership of Bruce Rioch and with fellow youngsters like Gary Pallister and Stuart Ripley, Cooper was ever-present as Boro won promotion from the Third Division at the first attempt and missed just one league game as the club completed a memorable rise into the top flight. But when relegation followed, injury and loss of form caused Cooper to spend spells out of the side and he was switched to right-back following the arrival of Jimmy Phillips for what turned out to be his last season at the club. The latter stages of Cooper's Boro career were marred by stress fractures in his right foot and when Lennie Lawrence took over as Boro manager it signalled the end of Cooper's time at the club.

In the summer of 1991, ex-manager Bruce Rioch snapped up his former charge for £300,000 and took him to Millwall. Rioch's successor Mick McCarthy was responsible for converting Cooper into a centre-back and his value soared before Frank Clark paid £1.5 million to take him to Nottingham Forest. In 1995, Cooper was picked to play for England against Sweden and Brazil - including Juninho - in the Umbro Cup to add to the eight under-21 caps he had earned while with Boro.

He may be better known as a centre-back at Nottingham Forest but Cooper was an impressive left-back in his five years with Boro.

BORO RECORD 1985-91

Season	Div	League App	League Gls	Cup App	Cup Gls	Total App	Total Gls
1985/86	2	9(2)	0	0(1)	0	9(3)	0
1986/87	3	46	0	12	1	58	1
1987/88	2	43	2	12	0	55	2
1988/89	1	35	2	7	1	42	3
1989/90	2	18(3)	2	9	1	27(3)	3
1990/91	2	32	0	10	0	42	0
Total		**183(5)**	**6**	**50(1)**	**3**	**233(6)**	**9**

England: 2 caps (none with Boro) 0 gls.

"When I played with him he was at left-back but has turned out to be an excellent centre-back as well. He's a reliable footballer who can also play in midfield and right-back. He's good in the air, a good tackler and a dedicated pro."
Stephen Pears.

"He was very good on the ball and a born leader. We had two or three of them at the time and all went on to become good captains."
Trevor Senior.

"A good defender who was and still is very good at going forward. He's stylish and packs a good shot. I remember him scoring a few good goals in one season with Boro."
Mark Burke.

MY TOP 5
Colin Cooper

1. Tony Mowbray
2. Bernie Slaven
3. Bryan Robson
4. Jim Platt
5. Willie Maddren

Cooper was a stylish performer as Boro's young side rose from the Third to First Division in the late 1980's.

Heine OTTO

" He had everything a midfielder should have "

Born: Amsterdam 24-08-54

In a struggling, mediocre Boro team, the tall Dutchman Heine Otto was a touch of class. Had Otto figured in one of the club's better sides, he would surely have been rightly remembered as one of the club's best ever attacking midfielders. The fact that he was top scorer in his first season with just five goals summed up the problems the club had in the early 80s.

Otto's professional career started in Holland with Twente Enschede. He had previously worked in his father-in-law's gold business and in a whisky distillery. Otto became the star of the Twente side when Dutch international Arnold Muhren left to become part of Bobby Robson's successful Ipswich team.

Otto capably filled the gap and earned several under-23 caps for his country. He was given just one chance to impress on the full international stage. He was a substitute 20 minutes from the end of a game with Yugoslavia but never added to his one cap.

In August 1981, Otto followed Muhren over the North Sea to join Middlesbrough. During the summer, Otto had played in three friendlies for Boro and manager Bobby Murdoch saw enough in the 26-year-old to make the move permanent. Otto made his debut in the first game of the 1981/82 season and made it a memorable debut with a goal. Sadly, Boro lost the match 3-1 to Spurs and, despite Otto's impressive performances, the team slipped out of the First Division.

Throughout the next three seasons, as Boro switched managers from Murdoch to Malcolm Allison to Willie Maddren and languished near the basement of the Second Division, Otto kept his place. His skilful play and regular goalscoring endeared him to the club's fans and they were left disappointed when he rejected a contract extension in May 1985 and returned to his homeland to join Second Division Den Haag. There, he set a Dutch record for successive appearances before becoming an executive with the club.After retiring, Otto moved into coaching and is now part of the famous Ajax youth set-up.

In the disappointing early 80s Boro team, Heine Otto was one of few stars to shine through with his performances in the midfield.

BORO RECORD 1981-85

Season	Div	League App	League Gls	Cup App	Cup Gls	Total App	Total Gls
1981/82	1	40	4	5	1	45	5
1982/83	2	40(2)	9	7	2	47(2)	11
1983/84	2	42	7	5	1	47	8
1984/85	2	41(1)	4	4	0	45(1)	4
Total		**163(3)**	**24**	**21**	**4**	**184(3)**	**28**

Holland: 1 cap (none with Boro) 0 gls.

MY TOP 5
Peter Beagrie

1. Heine Otto
2. Willie Maddren
3. David Mills
4. David Armstrong
5. Craig Johnston

Otto with Stephen Pears and a young mascot before a game against Manchester City at Ayresome Park in the 1983/84 season. He was to finish second top scorer in the campaign.

MY TOP 5
Heine Otto

1. Irving Nattrass
2. Kevin Beattie
3. Darren Wood
4. Stephen Bell
5. Mick Kennedy

"He was a gentle giant and a gentleman as well. He had great rapport with the kids at the club and was a great pro on and off the pitch. He put in some great performances as well as scoring a lot of goals. He was a big fella but with close control. He didn't shirk a tackle and caused problems in the air."
Peter Beagrie.

"Heine stood at 6ft 2in and he was classy and skilful with the ball which is unusual for someone of that height. He was class and had everything a midfielder should have."
Gary Hamilton.

Willie FERNIE

" He could make the ball talk "

Born: Kinglassie 22-11-30

Talented ball player Willie Fernie was a Scottish regular before moving south to Ayresome Park. The transfer came at the end of his international days but the skilful wing-forward proved to be a fine signing for his three years at the club.

Fernie, by then 28 years old, was recruited by Boro manager Bob Dennison from Celtic in December 1958. With the Scottish giants, Fernie had earned a regular slot in the Scotland side. His 12 caps spanned four years, starting with a World Cup qualifier against Finland in 1954 and included appearances in the 1954 and 1958 World Cup Finals in Switzerland and Sweden. In the 1954 competition he played in one of Scotland's heaviest defeats - 7-0 to Uruguay. His last international against Paraguay was in the 1958 finals - six months before his move to Boro. Fernie had also represented his country at league and B international level.

Bob Dennison paid out a substantial fee of £18,000 to take Fernie to Ayresome Park three months into the 1958/59 season. The fee matched the club's record transfer paid to take Bill Harris from Hull City four years earlier. Fernie made his Boro debut at inside-right against Ipswich in December 1958 and wore the number eight shirt for the remainder of the season and the following term. He scored his first goal in his fourth game - a 3-1 win over Huddersfield - but his return of three goals in his 22-month Boro career was disappointing.

Three games into the 1960/61 season, Dennison allowed Fernie to leave. He was transferred back to Celtic and played out the rest of his career at Parkhead. Fernie tried his hand at management with a spell in charge of Kilmarnock in 1974.

Talented Willie Fernie played in the 1958 World Cup for Scotland before signing for Boro.

BORO RECORD 1958-61

Season	Div	League App	Gls	Cup App	Gls	Total App	Gls
1958/59	2	23	2	1	0	24	2
1959/60	2	39	1	1	0	40	1
1960/61	2	3	0	1	0	4	0
Total		**65**	**3**	**3**	**0**	**68**	**3**

Scotland: 12 caps (0 with Boro) 1 gl.

Willie Fernie (middle row, second left) pictured with the Boro squad for the 1959/60 season. Seated below Fernie are internationals Brian Clough and Bill Harris.

"He was very skilful but also a great trainer. He worked all the time and was a great influence on me and all the other lads. He would even train with the juniors. He once said to me 'Never be seen with a pint glass in your hands, always be seen with a half'. "He was a real ambassador for football, coming from Celtic to Middlesbrough and even though he didn't play for too long he was an excellent footballer. He had the ball skills and was strong, he never hid on the pitch. He was the best inside-forward I played with "
Ray Yeoman.

"He was a hell of a schemer."
Bob Appleby.

"He was a great inside-forward, one of the best I've seen. He was a great ball-player but also had strength."
Dicky Robinson.

MY TOP 5
Ray Yeoman

1. Brian Clough
2. Willie Fernie
3. Bill Harris
4. Alan Peacock
5. John Hickton

Tony McANDREW

"A great defender and a winner"

Born: Lanark 11-04-56

It took Tony McAndrew five years to establish himself in the Middlesbrough side but he developed into a rugged, hard-working regular. In two spells with the club McAndrew notched up more than 350 games and also served the club as captain.

The former Scottish Youth international joined Boro in July 1971 but had to wait until November 1973 when he was asked to fill the boots of the injured Graeme Souness for the visit of Luton to Ayresome Park. He spent the rest of the promotion season on the sidelines and made another solitary appearance in the subsequent season, a year after his debut. It was not until the tail end of the 1975/76 season that McAndrew won a regular place in centre-defence. He occupied various positions in the side and was employed as a centre-forward, breaking his goal duck to devastating effect, with a hat-trick in a 3-0 win over Sheffield United in April 1976.

During the summer of 1976 McAndrew played for Vancouver Whitecaps in the North American Soccer League. He returned to cement his place in the Boro team and when Stuart Boam left in 1979, John Neal handed him the captaincy. In the summer of 1982, as Boro dropped out of the First Division, McAndrew turned down a contract offer and elected to join his former manager Neal at Chelsea. Boro demanded £300,000 but a tribunal set the fee at £92,500.

After two seasons at Stamford Bridge in which he played only 20 games, McAndrew was brought back to Ayresome Park by his former team-mate Willie Maddren. He was employed in defence for two years but when Boro dropped into the Third Division, McAndrew drifted out of the professional game. He made a belated return to league football late 1988 for short spells with Hartlepool and Darlington also turning out for Northern League Billingham Synthonia and Boro chairman Steve Gibson's side, Bulkhaul.

After coaching spells at Darlington and Hartlepool, he joined former Boro youth team coach Brian Little at Leicester and is currently coach alongside Little at Aston Villa.

Scotsman Tony McAndrew was a good club servant in two spells playing mostly in the centre of defence.

BORO RECORD 1973-84 & 86

Season	Div	League App	Gls	Cup App	Gls	Total App	Gls
1973/74	2	1	0	0	0	1	0
1974/75	1	1	0	0	0	1	0
1975/76	1	12	3	3(2)	0	15(2)	3
1976/77	1	38(1)	1	4(1)	1	42(2)	2
1977/78	1	41	0	8	1	49	1
1978/79	1	38	1	3	0	41	1
1979/80	1	39	1	6	0	45	1
1980/81	1	36(1)	3	6	0	42(1)	3
1981/82	1	39	4	5	0	44	4
1984/85	2	32	0	2	1	34	1
1985/86	2	34	2	5	0	39	2
Total		**311(2)**	**15**	**42(3)**		**353(5)**	**18**

Tony McAndrew (centre) could never be accused of giving less than 100% when he played for Boro.

"He was brilliant to play alongside, one of the most 100 per cent players I ever played with. He was a bit of a sod because he never shut up moaning but that was what we needed. I got lethargic at times but when you got the rough edge of Tony's tongue you soon got on with it. You used to do things just to shut him up. He was an inspirational leader."
Billy Ashcroft.

Tony McAndrew is the youngest player to score a hat-trick for Boro. He was just six days past his 20th birthday when he netted all three in a 3-0 win over Sheffield United in April 1976.

"He was one of the best pro's I have come across. He was a great winner with a tremendous outlook. He was a great defender - a very good tackler who played it simple. He set standards not just on the field but off it as well."
John Neal.

Jimmy GORDON

" A great tackler - firm but fair "

Born: Fauldhouse 23-10-15

When Newcastle United resumed football after the war they believed the best days of 30-year-old right-half Jimmy Gordon were firmly behind him. But the hard-tackling, ball-playing midfielder proved the Magpies wrong by playing on for another nine years in the top flight and proving to be an excellent servant for Middlesbrough.

Gordon joined Newcastle from Wishaw Juniors in April 1935 and went on to make 132 league appearances for the club. The outbreak of war, as with so many of Gordon's contemporaries, robbed him of his best years and when football resumed in late 1945, Newcastle decided to release their midfielder.

The words of one Newcastle director, who had described Gordon as 'a 20 minute footballer' were still ringing in his ears when Gordon made the journey south to Ayresome Park. Gordon immediately established himself in David Jack's Boro team, making his debut in the FA Cup in January 1946 before taking his place in the midfield for the first league campaign of 1946/47.

Gordon steadfastly proved Newcastle wrong by establishing himself as a regular over the next season alongside Mannion and Hardwick and he had passed the age of 36 before he became a more infrequent sight in the Boro side. Still, he remained with the club, capably stepping in when required, playing his last game in February 1954 at the age of 38.

After retiring from the game, Gordon had a spell in charge of Boro's junior side before moving to Blackburn Rovers to become the club's reserve team trainer. Former Boro team-mates Brian Clough and Peter Taylor brought in Gordon when they took charge at Derby County and he was trainer when the Rams won the league title in 1972. When the management duo moved on to Nottingham Forest, Gordon followed, seeing the club's European Cup triumph. He was also given the honour of leading Forest out for a League Cup Final. He died in 1996.

Jimmy Gordon became one of the most reliable post war Boro defenders.

BORO RECORD 1946-54

Season	Div	League App	Gls	Cup App	Gls	Total App	Gls
1945/46	1	-	-	6	1	6	1
1946/47	1	36	1	7	0	43	1
1947/48	1	35	0	3	0	38	0
1948/49	1	38	1	1	0	39	1
1949/50	1	38	1	4	0	42	1
1950/51	1	34	0	1	0	35	0
1951/52	1	30	0	0	0	30	0
1952/53	1	10	0	0	0	10	0
1953/54	1	10	0	0	0	10	0
Total		**231**	**3**	**22**	**1**	**253**	**4**

"Jimmy was a strong midfielder who I played behind during most of my time with Boro. When we were attacking down the right, he would go right to the dead ball line in the corner and I remember how I used to think 'if they break now they've got me two-on-one'. I can honestly say though that Jimmy was never caught out of position leaving me with his man as well as my own."
George Hardwick.

"He was as hard as they come, a great tackler - firm but fair. He was 5ft 4in tall but was a tremendous worker. He played left-half and I played right-half, if they got past us, they were lucky."
Harry Bell.

"Just what every club needs. He could win the ball and was a very good tackler."
Alex McCrae.

Watched by George Hardwick (centre), Jimmy Gordon (right) shepherds the ball back to keeper Dave Cumming during a match from the 1946/47 season.

Gordon JONES

" His left peg was magic "

Born: Sedgefield 06-03-43

When 15-year-old Gordon Jones signed on as an amateur for Boro in 1958, he started a 15-year spell with the club which saw him play more times for Boro than only other player since the war. His total of 527 appearances in league and cup leaves him second only to goalkeeper Tim Williamson in Boro's all-time list.

Jones signed professional forms in the month of his 17th birthday and made a sooner than expected debut in January 1961 on a trip to Southampton. He was the squad's 12th man when Boro made the journey to the Dell but Derek Stonehouse was taken ill and Jones stepped in at right-back.

When Boro returned to the South coast a week later to play Portsmouth, it was Jones rather than Stonehouse who started the game. Over the next couple of seasons, Jones switched between the flanks and it was the departure of Mick McNeil to Ipswich that saw him establish himself in the left-back slot that was to be his for most of the next decade.

Jones, capped at England Youth level, made his England under-23 debut in a 7-1 thrashing of Israel in November 1961 and the team were unbeaten in any of his nine appearances. He was in the frame for full honours around the time of the 1966 World Cup triumph but the form of Ray Wilson and Keith Newton placed them above Jones in Alf Ramsey's pecking order. Jones was instead picked for an under-23 tour but a cracked bone in his leg ruled him out.

When Boro slipped into Division Three in 1966, with the departure of Ian Gibson, Jones took over the captain's armband. He skippered the side to immediate promotion back into Division Two but he never saw top flight football with the club.

Jones was awarded a testimonial in 1969 and four years later, he moved on to finish his playing career with Darlington. He made 85 appearances for the Quakers before retiring in 1974 and moving into business in the Teesside area where he still lives today.

Gordon Jones lies second in Boro's all-time appearance list, turning out more than 500 times for the club.

BORO RECORD 1960-73

Season	Div	League App	League Gls	Cup App	Cup Gls	Total App	Total Gls
1960/61	2	17	0	1	0	18	0
1961/62	2	38	0	6	0	44	0
1962/63	2	36	0	5	0	41	0
1963/64	2	29	1	3	0	32	1
1964/65	2	41	1	5	0	46	1
1965/66	2	42	0	4	0	46	0
1966/67	3	40(2)	1	7	0	47(2)	1
1967/68	2	41	1	8	0	49	1
1968/69	2	38	0	3	0	41	0
1969/70	2	42	0	10	0	52	0
1970/71	2	41	0	5	1	46	1
1971/72	2	34	0	8	0	42	0
1972/73	2	18(3)	0	5	0	23(3)	0
Total		**457(5)**	**4**	**70**	**1**	**527(5)**	**5**

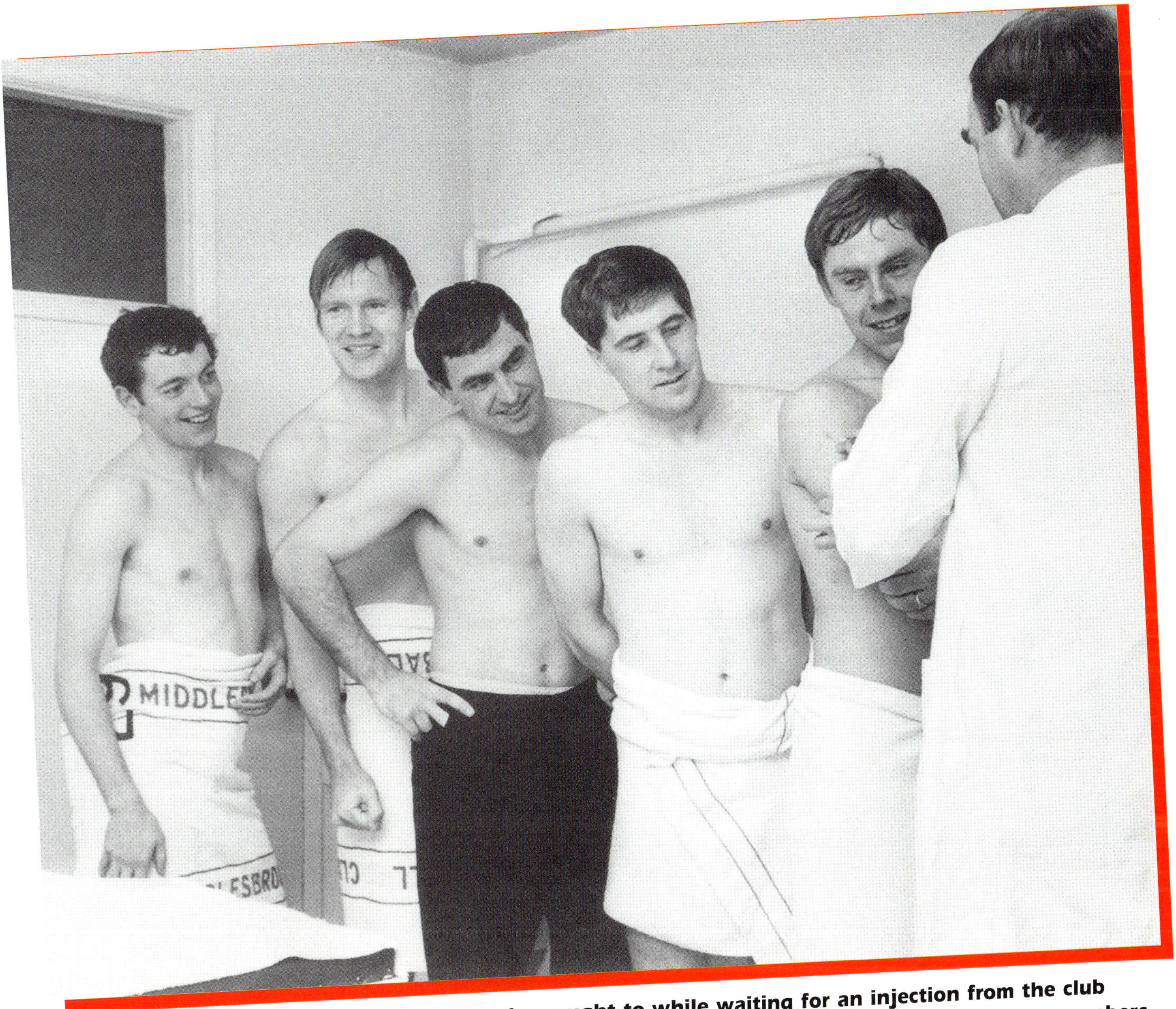

The Boro players look more cheerful than they ought to while waiting for an injection from the club doctor in the late 1960s. Jones looks on from his place of third in the queue, along with other members of Boro's Best Eric McMordie (left) and John Hickton (second left).

"I only played with him for about two years but he had a terrific left foot and was ideal for the way we played because he was an outlet on the left wing and he was so accurate with his long balls. He used to come up from left-back and take corners which in those days was unheard of. If he was playing today, he would probably have made a great wing-back."
Hugh McIlmoyle.

"My old mate Jonesy had the best left peg I have ever seen. His right wasn't up to much but it was a pleasure to see him hit the ball with his left foot."
Billy Horner.

"His left peg was magic. He could put the ball in anywhere."
Willie Whigham.

MY TOP 5
Gordon Jones

1. Bill Harris
2. Graeme Souness
3. Hugh McIlmoyle
4. Juninho
5. Alan Peacock

Curtis FLEMING

" One of the best defenders in the Premiership "

Born: Manchester 08-10-68

Boro paid just £50,000 to pluck Curtis Fleming from Irish part-timers St Patrick's Athletic. Six years on, looking more than comfortable among a team of million pound stars, Fleming has proved one of the club's most astute signings.

Manager Colin Todd spotted the potential of the young full-back and, despite Todd's departure in the summer of 1991, the new manager Lennie Lawrence went ahead with the deal. Fleming made his debut as a substitute against Ipswich in August 1991 but first team opportunities were initially restricted. But when regular right-back Gary Parkinson was injured he stepped in as the team challenged successfully for promotion to the Premier League. Fleming was also asked to step in when Parkinson failed a fitness test for Boro's visit to Manchester United in the semi-finals of the League Cup.

The arrival of Chris Morris from Celtic provided a contest for the right-back slot in the top flight and injuries have often prevented Boro making full use of Fleming's ability. The £1 m signing of right-back Neil Cox also forced Fleming to show his versatility by switching from his natural position at right-back to the left side where he has comfortably played most of his games in recent seasons. Since promotion into the Premier League, Fleming has overcome a career threatening injury and become noted for his fine supporting runs down the flanks as well as excellent tackling and marking. He is rated as one of the best full-backs in the league by Bryan Robson. The manager showed his faith in Fleming by providing him with a five-year contract that committed him to the Riverside until 2001.

After picking up one under 21-cap and being selected at B level during his time with St. Patricks, Fleming earned his first cap for the Republic of Ireland as a substitute for Denis Irwin against the Czech Republic in April 1996. That month also saw him break his long goal duck - almost five years after his Boro debut - when he netted in a 2-1 defeat at the hands of Wimbledon at the Cellnet Riverside Stadium. He has since gone on to win a number of full caps alongside his Boro team-mate Alan Moore and has also been a key member of the first Boro side to reach a major cup final.

Curtis Fleming was a bargain buy whose Boro career has seen great changes at the club.

BORO RECORD 1991-

Season	Div	League App	Gls	Cup App	Gls	Total App	Gls
1991/92	2	23(5)	0	3(2)	0	26(7)	0
1992/93	P	22(2)	0	3	0	25(2)	0
1993/94	1	31(5)	0	7(1)	0	38(6)	0
1994/95	1	21	0	6	0	28	0
1995/96	P	13	1	2	0	15	1
1996/97	P	26	0	10	1	36	1
Total		**136(12)**	**1**	**31(3)**	**1**	**168(15)**	**2**

Republic of Ireland: 7 caps (all with Boro) 0 gls.

*Figures correct to 9.4.97

MY TOP 5
Curtis Fleming

1. Bernie Slaven
2. Juninho
3. Gary Pallister
4. Emerson
5. John Hendrie

"I respect Curtis for the way he came from Ireland where he had played for part-timers in St Patrick's and has eventually established himself as one of the best defenders in the Premiership."
Keith O'Halloran.

"I respect Curtis for his positive attitude and 100 per cent approach to the game. You can always expect nothing short of 100 per cent from Curtis no matter where he is asked to play. He is also a very nice guy off the pitch. He hasn't let his success go to his head like some people do."
Mikkel Beck.

"He'll tackle brick walls and take on rhinos for the team. He doesn't care where his foot or head goes, he'll put it in there if needs be"
Craig HIgnett.

"Curtis is an excellent full-back. He is a very good marker and tackler who also gives good support to the front players"
Vladimir Kinder.

They may be team-mates now but back in August 1996, when Boro took on Inter Milan in a benefit match for Willie Maddren at the Cellnet Riverside Stadium, there was no love lost between Curtis Fleming and Gianluca Festa.

Dave CUMMING

" An outstanding goalkeeper "

Born: Aberdeen 06-05-10

For a goalkeeper who played his last game more than half a century ago, Dave Cumming's appearance among Boro's best is quite an achievement, especially considering he played only 157 first team games for the club. But Cumming was a talented keeper, much respected by his team-mates, who disproved the theory about dodgy Scottish goalkeepers.

Cumming was first choice between the sticks for three full seasons before the outbreak of World War II at the start of his fourth season at Ayresome Park. He was still the club's regular number one when league football resumed after a seven-year gap. By then, however, he was 36 years old and in the twilight of his career. But for the war, he would surely have made closer to 400 appearances for the club.

Cumming signed for Boro in a £3,000 deal - then a record for a Scottish-based goalkeeper - early in the 1936/37 campaign after Grimsby keeper Jim Tweedy had turned down a move to Ayresome Park. He had previously played for Aberdeen before making a name for himself at Arbroath. Despite conceding eight goals in his first two Boro appearances, he went on to become a big crowd favourite with his brave and athletic goalkeeping displays. He was the last line of a talented Boro defence which included Bobby Baxter, George Laking, Bobby Stuart and Billy Forrest.

His displays for Boro won him a deserved call-up to the Scotland team and he won what turned out to be his one and only cap against England at Wembley in April 1938. Despite keeping a clean sheet in a shock 1-0 win, Cumming was not selected for any of his country's four remaining internationals before the outbreak of war, though he did play in a war-time 6-2 defeat, also against England at Wembley, in 1944. Ironically, his Boro team-mate Micky Fenton made his one and only England appearance in the opposing team at Wembley in 1938.

After guesting for Newcastle United during the war, he returned to the Boro side in 1946/47, the first football league campaign after the war. However, it was to be his last for the club. Typical of the man, he did not bow out quietly. In one of his final games, he punched Arsenal's Leslie Compton after a goalmouth scramble. Before the referee had even made his inevitable decision to dismiss him, Cumming had handed his keeper's jersey to Johnny Spuhler and walked off the pitch.

Goalkeeper Dave Cumming, whose career spanned the Second World War, is rated by many as Boro's best ever number one.

BORO RECORD 1936-47

Season	Div	League App	League Gls	Cup App	Cup Gls	Total App	Total Gls
1936/37	1	32	0	1	0	33	0
1937/38	1	28	0	3	0	31	0
1938/39	1	38	0	4	0	42	0
1945/46	-	-	-	7	0	7	0
1946/47	1	37	0	7	0	44	0
Total		**135**	**0**	**22**	**0**	**157**	**0**

Scotland: 1 cap(with Boro)

MY TOP 5
Derek Stonehouse

1. Dave Cumming
2. George Hardwick
3. Bob Baxter
4. Wilf Mannion
5. Brian Clough

"A strong-minded Scotsman who was a fine goalkeeper for Boro."
Ralph Birkett.

"I was very young at the time Cumming played in goal for Boro but I don't think we've ever had a really outstanding goalkeeper apart from him. I still remember the day we played Arsenal and Leslie Compton mowed him down without even attempting to get the ball. Cumming just stood up and chinned him - and off he went! But from what I saw of him he was Boro's finest goalkeeper."
Derek Stonehouse.

The unlikely sight of Scotsman Cumming (centre, front) surrounded by team-mates in England shirts came from a war-time charity game. The team wore George Camsell's England shirts for the match at Ayresome Park in 1943. Camsell is to Cumming's left and Camsell's son is at the keeper's feet.

Eric McMORDIE

" A great midfielder who could run a game "

Born: Belfast 12-04-46

But for a bout of homesickness, Eric McMordie could have been a member of the great Manchester United side of the late 1960's. Instead, he became an integral part of a very impressive Boro side who were never quite good enough to climb out of the old Second Division. Consequently, McMordie - whose Christian name was actually Alexander - spent his entire career outside the top flight when his talents would have fitted in easily at the highest level.

Spotted by Manchester United as a youngster in Belfast, 15-year-old McMordie had a short trial at Old Trafford with fellow Irish youngster George Best. Both returned to Ireland feeling homesick but, while Best was persuaded to return for a second spell, McMordie stayed in Ireland. The rest, as they say is history. However, the young McMordie did well enough for local amateur side Dundela to earn a recommendation to Boro manager Raich Carter from the club's Irish-based scout, Matt Willis, and joined Boro as a professional in September 1964.

It was not until September of the following year that he made his first team debut at inside-forward against Plymouth but he became an immediate hit by scoring on his home debut in a 4-0 win over Rotherham United. However, the season ended in relegation to the Third Division for the first time in Boro's history and McMordie initially struggled to establish himself in Stan Anderson's rejuvenated team. However, he became an important member of the team in a midfield role over the next six seasons and won the first of 21 caps for Northern Ireland against Israel in 1968.

Although initially part of Jack Charlton's successful side of 1973/74, he made way for Bobby Murdoch on the Scot's arrival from Celtic and it quickly became clear he had no future at Ayresome Park. A loan spell with Sheffield Wednesday which brought six goals in nine games, surprisingly failed to end in a permanent deal. He had not started a first team game for the club for over 17 months when he signed for York City in May 1975. Although still in his 20s, McMordie's career was in decline and he moved on to Hartlepool after just 42 league games at Bootham Crescent. He made a further 46 appearances for Hartlepool before ending his playing days at the early age of just 31. He has continued to live and work on Teesside since his retirement.

Young Irishman Eric McMordie almost joined Manchester United with his friend George Best but instead became an important member of the Boro side.

BORO RECORD 1965-74

Season	Div	League		Cup		Total	
		App	Gls	App	Gls	App	Gls
1965/66	2	17	4	4	1	21	5
1966/67	3	19	0	3	0	22	0
1967/68	2	29(1)	1	1(1)	1	30(2)	2
1968/69	2	39	6	3	0	42	6
1969/70	2	28(4)	3	9	2	37(4)	5
1970/71	2	30(3)	1	4	0	34(3)	1
1971/72	2	36(1)	3	6	0	42(1)	3
1972/73	2	26	4	5	0	31	4
1973/74	2	7(1)	0	0	0	7(1)	0
Total		**231(10)**	**22**	**35(1)**	**4**	**266(11)**	**26**

Northern Ireland: 21 caps (all with Boro), 3 gls.

McMordie swivels to get in a shot against Orient at Ayresome Park in the early 1970s. He scored 26 times in his Boro career.

"Before Souness arrived, Eric, another midfielder, was my hero from when I watched Boro as a kid. Eric could run a game and had his best season when Boro got promoted from the Third Division."
Chris Kamara.

"He had the ability to go by people. He was an international in his own right and also had that charisma. He was very effective on the pitch and could win games for you."
Colin Todd.

"Of all the players I was with at Middlesbrough, Eric made a marked impression on me. He showed the importance of being professional but also enjoying yourself. Whether it be on the pitch or in training, he always had time for a laugh or a joke. He was also a great midfield player who could get forward and back. You can't argue with the number of caps he got."
David Armstrong.

Mick McNEIL

" He was a class full-back or centre-half "

Born: Middlesbrough 07-02-40

Robust defender Mick McNeil never played in the First Division with Middlesbrough but his displays were impressive enough to make him one of only two Boro players to win caps for England in the 1960s. The sturdy full-back was a regular through the latter days of Bob Dennison's managerial stint at the club and was unfortunate never to make it into the top flight at Ayresome Park.

McNeil was signed by Boro coach Jimmy Gordon in May 1957. He had earlier played for Middlesbrough Boys and had been spotted turning out for the Cargo Fleet works team.

He made his Boro debut at left-half in December 1958 in a 6-4 victory against Brighton. but competition for places restricted McNeil's involvement to a handful of appearances in his first season. It was in the following 1959/60 campaign that McNeil established his place at full-back, wearing the number three shirt in every game that term.

McNeil's name was an infrequent sight on the Boro score-sheet during his six-year stint with the club. He had to wait more than two years after his debut before notching his first goal in a 2-2 draw with Charlton at Ayresome Park in March 1961. It was to be one of just three goals for the club.

But it was his defensive qualities that earned McNeil the plaudits. International recognition came relatively quickly when England under-23 caps followed an appearance for an FA XI against the Army. He then made his full England debut in November 1960 in a 5-1 victory over Wales. He went on to make nine appearances for his country, his last in a World Cup qualifier against Luxembourg at Wembley in September 1961. But he failed to make the squad for the 1962 World Cup Finals in Chile.

Two years later, McNeil left Boro to join Ipswich Town. He helped the club to promotion in 1968 and retired three years later. He now lives in Bury St Edmunds and runs a sports retail business.

Mick McNeil won nine international caps while a Second Division player with Boro.

BORO RECORD 1958-64

Season	Div	League App	Gls	Cup App	Gls	Total App	Gls
1958/59	2	7	0	0	0	7	0
1959/60	2	42	0	1	0	43	0
1960/61	2	39	1	2	0	41	1
1961/62	2	38	1	7	0	45	1
1962/63	2	32	1	4	0	36	1
1963/64	2	20	0	1	0	21	0
Total		**178**	**3**	**15**	**0**	**193**	**3**

England: 9 caps (all with Boro) 0 gls.

McNeil revisits the scene of former glories and receives applause from the gathered Boro fans for the final game at Ayresome Park.

MY TOP 5
Mick McNeil

1. Wilf Mannion
2. Juninho
3. Brian Clough
4. Graeme Souness
5. Alan Peacock

"He was a very good defender, a good header of the ball, had two good feet, was mobile and could play either side at full-back. I would also say he was the best centre-back at the club while I was there."
Bryan Phillips.

"He was a class full-back or centre-back. You could rely on him until your dying day. He never had a bad game."
Bob Appleby.

"Mick was at the club when I arrived. He won a number of England caps and he was a player who never panicked."
Arthur Horsfield.

MY TOP 5
Bob Appleby

1. Brian Clough
2. Bill Harris
3. Cyril Knowles
4. Mick McNeil
5. Willie Fernie

John O'ROURKE

" A great finisher "

Born: Northampton 11-02-45

"Give us a goal John O'Rourke", came the cry from the Holgate throughout Boro's promotion campaign from Division Three during the 1966/67 season.

O'Rourke had arrived at Ayresome Park from Luton Town with an excellent scoring record of 64 goals in 84 games after previous spells as an amateur with Chelsea and a brief time at Arsenal.

His Boro career got off to flyer with a brace of goals on his debut in a 3-2 win over Colchester and although he had to wait until the end of September for his next goal, he enjoyed a season of high personal triumph.

He finished the campaign on 30 goals which included three hat tricks. His finest hour was without doubt the final game of the season against Oxford United at Ayresome Park. Boro required nothing less than victory to secure promotion back to Division Two and with a crowd officially given as 40,000 but more like 50,000 O'Rourke was in blistering form. He hammered home a hat-trick which inspired Boro to a powerful 4-1 victory and sent Stan Anderson to promotion in his first full season in charge of the club.

At the end of the season, O'Rourke was rewarded for his excellent form when he was awarded an England under-23 cap against Turkey in Ankara and, true to form, he was on target once again.

Back in Division Two Boro had an indifferent start and O'Rourke only bagged one goal in his first seven games. However, between the end of September and Christmas he fired home 11 goals, including two further hat-tricks against Derby and Carlisle.

With his marvellous goalscoring ratio, it was only going to be a matter of time before envious eyes were cast towards Middlesbrough and in February 1968 Bobby Robson stepped in to sign O'Rourke for First Division Ipswich Town.

His stay at Portman Road was brief and he was on the move again 18 months later to Coventry City where he was again productive on the goalscoring front. Further moves followed to QPR and Bournemouth before he retired in 1975. He is now settled back on the south coast where he runs his own retail store.

Training at Ayresome Park, O'Rourke shows the poise that brought him plenty of goals in a lethal partnership with John Hickton.

BORO RECORD 1966-68

Season	Div	League App	League Gls	Cup App	Cup Gls	Total App	Total Gls
1966/67	3	39	27	4	3	43	30
1967/68	2	25	11	4	1	29	12
Total		**64**	**38**	**8**	**4**	**72**	**42**

John O'Rourke (back row, fourth from the right) pictured with the full Boro squad for their first season in the Third Division in 1966/67.

MY TOP 5
Don Masson

1. Brian Clough
2. John Hickton
3. John O'Rourke
4. Graeme Souness
5. Juninho

"Along with John Hickton, he was pretty ordinary as an individual but they struck it off as a combination. They were both great finishers."
Don Masson.

MY TOP 5
John O'Rourke

1. Brian Clough
2. John Hickton
3. David Chadwick
4. Willie Whigham
5. Derrick Downing

"When I was only a young lad, my next door neighbour used to take me to see the Boro play and John O'Rourke was my first hero. I recall going to watch the reserves every other Saturday in those days as well."
Mark Proctor.

Hugh McILMOYLE

" An exceptional header of the ball "

Born: Cambuslang 29-01-40

Rated by many as the best header of the ball ever to play for Boro, Hughie McIlmoyle was a football journeyman who won a place in the hearts of all Middlesbrough fans who saw him play. McIlmoyle was an extremely talented forward who manager Stan Anderson believed could shoot Boro into the First Division. It remains one of Stan's regrets that he failed to get the best out of McIlmoyle on a consistent basis.

McIlmoyle was an immediate hit when he broke into the Leicester City team during the 1960-61 campaign, scoring four goals in his first seven games, but failed to maintain that early momentum despite appearing in the 1961 League Cup Final against Spurs moved on to Rotherham United in 1962. Just 12 games later he was on the move again, this time to Carlisle United where he wrote his name into the record books as the country's top scorer in 1963/64, netting 39 goals in just 45 Fourth Division games.

A move to Wolves followed where he was a consistent goalscorer for three seasons. After a short spell at Bristol City, he returned to Carlisle for more scoring exploits. Middlesbrough became his sixth club in September 1969 when he linked up with John Hickton in the Boro forward line. He is particularly remembered by supporters for his inspiring performance in a 6-2 win over QPR in September 1970 when Boro came from two goals behind. However, Boro narrowly missed promotion in his first season at Ayresome Park and were again out of luck in 1970/71 despite a 15-goal contribution from McIlmoyle. In July 1971, he joined Preston North End, and later played for Morton before spending a third spell at Carlisle.

Despite not being the tallest striker in Boro's history, Hugh McIlmoyle was renowned for his outstanding ability in the air.

1969-71

Season	Div	League App	League Gls	Cup App	Cup Gls	Total App	Total Gls
1969-70	2	29	6	7	1	36	7
1970-71	2	40(1)	13	5	2	45(1)	15
Total		**69(1)**	**19**	**12**	**3**	**81(1)**	**22**

Much-travelled striker Hugh McIlmoyle was the man Boro manager Stan Anderson hoped would bring the goals needed to take Boro into the First Division.

Hugh McIlmoyle broke his nose in his Boro debut and was detained overnight in North Riding Infirmary. To rub salt in the wound, Boro lost 2-0 to Blackpool.

MY TOP 5
Hugh McIlmoyle

1. Willie Maddren
2. Frank Spraggon
3. John Hickton
4. Gordon Jones
5. Bill Gates

"When you talk about Hugh McIlmoyle you talk about heading ability. I never saw John Charles but they reckon he had unbelievable heading ability and Hugh's timing was out of this world. You knew that if you were under pressure you could knock the ball up to him and he would win it nine times out of 10, then have the ability to direct it down to one of his own players. He was able to hang in the air while he was also clever on the floor. He was a very good target man."
Frank Spraggon.

"As can be seen with Everton and Duncan Ferguson at the moment, there is always room in football for a target man up front. Hugh was an exceptional header of the ball considering he was only about 5'10" but he had excellent timing. He also had a lot of skill and was an intelligent player but unfortunately I don't think some Boro fans realised just how good he was because he didn't stay long enough at the club. I remember our former coach Ian McFarlane telling us that he'd worked with Hugh when he was a youngster and he rated him as good as anybody he'd ever seen."
Gordon Jones.

MY TOP 5
Frank Spraggon

1. Graeme Souness
2. Juninho
3. Hugh McIlmoyle
4. Bobby Murdoch
5. Bill Harris

Cyril KNOWLES

" A classy player who was quick and strong "

Born: Fitzwilliam 13-07-44

"Nice one Cyril, nice one son!" So went the song which was inspired by Cyril Knowles during his hey-day with Tottenham Hotspur.

Although he made only 39 appearances for Boro between 1962 and 1964, Knowles left a big enough impression to inscribe himself as one of Boro's finest.

After spells as a youngster with Manchester United and Wolves, for whom his brother Peter played first division football for, Cyril joined Boro as an amateur after contacting Harold Shepherdson. His debut came in 1962 in a 3-3 draw with Derby as a replacement for the injured Mick McNeil at left back.

Knowles excelled in Boro's defence over the next season with his cultured displays as an attacking full-back and he soon caught the attention of Tottenham boss Bill Nicholson.

He moved to White Hart Lane in May 1964 for £45,000, then a record for a full-back and went on to earn England caps at under-23 and full level.

He remained with Spurs until he retired through a knee injury at the age of 31 in 1975 and during his time there he won many of the game's major honours. Without doubt he was one of Spurs' finest ever defenders.

After a brief spell coaching Doncaster, Cyril returned to Ayresome Park to work with Bobby Murdoch before taking on the managership of Darlington in 1983. He worked a great job at Feethams, leading the club to promotion in 1985.

In 1987 he took over at Torquay and enjoyed relative success there before once again returning to the North-east with Hartlepool where he proved a steadying influence and turned them into promotion contenders.

Sadly, Cyril was found to be suffering from a brain tumour in early 1991 and after a brave battle he sadly passed away on August 31st that year.

Nice hairstyle! Cyril Knowles oozed class from the moment he broke into the Boro side and although he played just 39 times he is still rated among Boro's Best.

1962-64

Season	Div	League App	League Gls	Cup App	Cup Gls	Total App	Total Gls
1962-63	2	9	0	0	0	9	0
1963-64	2	28	0	2	0	30	0
Total		**37**	**0**	**2**	**0**	**39**	**0**

England: 4 caps (none with Boro) 0 gls.

Cyril Knowles (front row, second left) pictured here with the famous Spurs side of 1964/65, developed into one of the country's leading full backs winning four full international caps for England.

"Cyril was a good full-back. It was clear to see from the first time I saw him play in a trialists match that he would go on to big things. He was a very classy player who was quick and strong. I think you could compare him to Stuart Pearce in the current game."
Arthur Horsfield.

"He was a class defender for Middlesbrough."
Bob Appleby.

MY TOP 5
Lennie Lawrence

1. Wilf Mannion
2. George Hardwick
3. Graeme Souness
4. Gary Pallister
5. Craig Johnston

MY TOP 5
Arthur Horsfield

1. Brian Clough
2. Alan Peacock
3. Cyril Knowles
4. Mick McNeil
5. Ian Gibson

Cyril Knowles was manager of Darlington when Gary Pallister had a loan spell at Feethams. The idea behind the loan move was to toughen up a professional newcomer in a lower division. Knowles spotted Pallister's potential and made a tongue-in-cheek £15,000 offer "to take the boy off your hands". Boro boss Willie Maddren politely refused the bid.

John CRAGGS

" A classy full-back with a sweet right foot "

Born: Flinthill 31-10-48

Strong tackling defender John Craggs' career was transformed when Stan Anderson splashed out £60,000 to take him to Ayresome Park. Craggs had spent six years at Newcastle but had made just 50 first team appearances due to the commanding form of United's Irish international David Craig. The switch from Tyneside to Teesside, however, was the launch-pad for an 11 year Boro career that would make Craggs one of the club's most loyal servants.

Craggs signed for Boro in a then club record deal in August 1971 after Hugh McIlmoyle had been sold to pay for the transfer. Craggs immediately donned the number two shirt that was to be his for the next decade. He was renowned for his attacking play from right-back as well as his defensive skills and his long throws into the opposition penalty areas are also remembered by many who saw him play. Having played a leading part in the promotion success of 1974 he became a mainstay at Boro through the First Division days under Jack Charlton.

By the summer of 1982, soon after a testimonial game against Newcastle, which featured Kevin Keegan amongst others, Craggs returned to St James' Park on a free transfer. He had notched up a tally of Boro appearances that leaves him in the top five of Boro's servants.

Craggs later enjoyed a spell as youth team coach at Hartlepool and currently works for Sport & Ski at the Teesside Retail Park in Middlesbrough.

Defender John Craggs was a record signing when he left Newcastle to join Boro but the club got a full return for the expenditure with 11 years good service.

BORO RECORD 1971-82

Season	Div	League App	Gls	Cup App	Gls	Total App	Gls
1971/72	2	38	2	8	1	46	3
1972/73	2	41	1	5	0	46	1
1973/74	2	39	3	5	0	44	3
1974/75	1	41	1	13	0	54	1
1975/76	1	36	1	17	1	53	2
1976/77	1	42	1	9	0	51	1
1977/78	1	37	2	7	0	44	2
1978/79	1	41	0	4	0	45	0
1979/80	1	42	1	6	0	48	1
1980/81	1	28(1)	0	3	0	31(1)	0
1981/82	1	23	0	2	0	25	0
Total		**408(1)**	**12**	**79**	**2**	**487(1)**	**14**

"John had great speed and passing ability. He would have made a great wing-back in the game today."
John Hickton.

"John was a good buy from Newcastle. He was an attacking full-back who would do well in the present game. We concentrated more on his defensive strengths because that was more essential at the time. He was strong and quick for a big lad and a good buy for £60,000. He was a good passer of the long and short ball and if he'd played for one of the bigger clubs he would have received more recognition."
Stan Anderson.

"My old partner on the right-hand side. We never fell out as many people said we did and he was a good player. I never saw many people skin John. He was quick, he got back and showed forwards away from the goal while he was very good going forward. John was a good overlapper who was not afraid to take a chance. I always say a defender's first job is to defend and John did that."
Terry Cochrane.

MY TOP 5
John Craggs

1. Graeme Souness
2. Willie Maddren
3. Brian Clough
4. Bobby Murdoch
5. David Armstrong

Craggs battles for possession with Wolves' Mel Eves at Molineaux during the 1980/81 season.

"A classy full-back and while people often say players had a sweet left foot, they rarely say it about right-footed players. John Craggs had a sweet right foot. He was a very good striker of the ball."
Peter Johnson.

MY TOP 5
Peter Johnson

1. Graeme Souness
2. Willie Maddren
3. Terry Cooper
4. Mark Proctor
5. John Craggs

Is this BORO'S BEST TEAM?

PEARS

PALLISTER

MOWBRAY

MADDREN

EMERSON

SOUNESS

ARMSTRONG

JUNINHO

MANNION

CLOUGH

SLAVEN

Subs: Ugolini, Hardwick, Murdoch, Hickton, Ravanelli

Team based on the results of the players' poll.

A Bunch of Fives

The Top Five Managers?

Number of Boro's Best players signed or given debuts by the Boro bosses.

1 Stan Anderson (1966-73) - 9
2 Bob Dennison (1954-63) - 7
3 Bryan Robson (1994-) - 5
4 David Jack (1944-52) - 4
5 Willie Maddren (1984-86) - 4

Top Five Signed/Given Debut by Stan Anderson

1 Graeme Souness
2 Willie Maddren
3 David Armstrong
4 John Hickton
5 Stuart Boam

Top Five Signed/Given Debut by Bob Dennison

1 Brian Clough
2 Alan Peacock
3 Ian Gibson
4 Willie Fernie
5 Gordon Jones

Top Five Signed/Given Debut by Bryan Robson

1 Juninho
2 Emerson
3 Fabrizio Ravanelli
4 Bryan Robson
5 Nick Barmby

Top Five Signed/Given Debut by David Jack

1 Dicky Robinson
2 Alex McCrae
3 Rolando Ugolini
4 Jimmy Gordon
5 Lindy Delapenha

Top Five Signed/Given Debut by Willie Maddren

1 Gary Pallister
2 Stephen Pears
3 Bernie Slaven
4 Stuart Ripley
5 David Mills (second spell)

Top Five Goalkeepers

1 Stephen Pears
2 Rolando Ugolini
3 Jim Platt
4 Dave Cumming
5 Willie Whigham

Top Five Full-Backs

1 George Hardwick
2 Dicky Robinson
3 Terry Cooper
4 Colin Cooper
5 Gordon Jones

Top Five Centre-Backs

1 Gary Pallister
2 Willie Maddren
3 Tony Mowbray
4 Bob Baxter
5 Stuart Boam

A Bunch of Fives

Top Five Forwards

1 Wilf Mannion
2 Brian Clough
3 Bernie Slaven
4 John Hickton
5 Fabrizio Ravanelli

Top Five English Internationals

1 Gary Pallister
2 Wilf Mannion
3 Brian Clough
4 David Armstrong
5 George Hardwick

Top Five Uncapped Stars

1 Willie Maddren
2 Tony Mowbray
3 Stephen Pears
4 Emerson
5 John Hickton

Top Five Teessiders

1 Wilf Mannion
2 Willie Maddren
3 Brian Clough
4 Tony Mowbray
5 George Hardwick

Top Five Scotsmen

1 Graeme Souness
2 Bobby Murdoch
3 John Hendrie
4 Bob Baxter
5 Alex McCrae

Top Five Players who cost Boro nothing

1 Gary Pallister
2 Wilf Mannion
3 Willie Maddren
4 Brian Clough
5 Tony Mowbray

Top Five Pre-War Players

1 Wilf Mannion
2 Bob Baxter
3 Micky Fenton
4 George Camsell
5 Dave Cumming

Top Five 40's Players

1 Wilf Mannion
2 George Hardwick
3 Micky Fenton
4 Dicky Robinson
5 Alex McCrae

Top Five 60's Players

1 Brian Clough
2 John Hickton
3 Bill Harris
4 Alan Peacock
5 Ian Gibson

Top Five 70's Players

1 Graeme Souness
2 Willie Maddren
3 David Armstrong
4 John Hickton
5 Bobby Murdoch

Top Five 80's Players

1 Gary Pallister
2 Tony Mowbray
3 Stephen Pears
4 Bernie Slaven
5 David Armstrong

Top Five 90's Players

1 Juninho
2 Tony Mowbray
3 Stephen Pears
4 Bernie Slaven
5 Emerson

Top Five Current Players

1 Juninho
2 Emerson
3 Fabrizio Ravanelli
4 Bryan Robson
5 Robbie Mustoe

Most appearances among Boro's Best

1 Gordon Jones - 532
2 John Hickton - 499
3 John Craggs - 488
4 Jim Platt - 481
5 George Camsell - 453

Least appearances among Boro's Best

1 Bryan Robson
2 Fabrizio Ravanelli
3 Emerson
4 Cyril Knowles
5 Nick Barmby

Least appearances excluding current players

1 Cyril Knowles - 39
2 Nick Barmby - 49
3 Willie Fernie - 68
4 John O'Rourke - 72
5 Craig Johnston - 78

Players' Bunches of Fives

PETER DAVENPORT
1 Juninho
2 Emerson
3 Brian Clough
4 David Armstrong
5 Gary Pallister

TREVOR SENIOR
1 Gary Pallister
2 Tony Mowbray
3 Colin Cooper
4 Stuart Ripley
5 Steve Pears

ARCHIE STEPHENS
1 Gary Pallister
2 Tony McAndrew
3 Tony Mowbray
4 Wilf Mannion
5 Steve Pears

PHIL WHELAN
1 Gary Pallister
2 Graeme Souness
3 Emerson
4 Craig Johnston
5 Juninho

NOBBY STILES
1 Wilf Mannion
2 Graeme Souness
3 Bobby Murdoch
4 Brian Clough
5 Willie Maddren

COLIN TODD
1 Brian Clough
2 Graeme Souness
3 Gary Pallister
4 Bobby Murdoch
5 Eric McMordie

ARTHUR HORSFIELD
1 Brian Clough
2 Alan Peacock
3 Cyril Knowles
4 Mick McNeil
5 Ian Gibson

BEN ROBERTS
1 Stephen Pears
2 John Hendrie
3 Juninho
4 Gary Pallister
5 Colin Cooper

NICKY MOHAN
1 Steve Pears
2 Gary Pallister
3 Tony Mowbray
4 Bernie Slaven
5 Gary Hamilton

JIMMY PHILLIPS
1 Steve Pears
2 Tony Mowbray
3 Stuart Ripley
4 Bernie Slaven
5 Ian Baird

IAN IRONSIDE
1 Steve Pears
2 Gary Pallister
3 Tony Mowbray
4 Bernie Slaven
5 Juninho

ALAN COMFORT
1 Bernie Slaven
2 Graeme Souness
3 Tony Mowbray
4 David Armstrong
5 Steve Pears

PAUL WILKINSON
1 Wilf Mannion
2 Bernie Slaven
3 Tony Mowbray
4 John Hendrie
5 Juninho

MALCOLM SMITH
1 Graeme Souness
2 David Armstrong
3 Willie Maddren
4 Fabrizio Ravanelli
5 John Hickton

MY TOP 5
MIKKEL BECK
1 Graeme Souness
2 Gary Pallister
3 John Hendrie
4 Juninho
5 Curtis Fleming

MY TOP 5
BRUCE RIOCH
1 Wilf Mannion
2 Brian Clough
3 Graeme Souness
4 Fabrizio Ravanelli
5 Juninho

VLADIMIR KINDER
1 Juninho
2 Emerson
3 Fabrizio Ravanelli
4 Curtis Fleming
5 Robbie Mustoe

STEVE VICKERS
1 Fabrizio Ravanelli
2 Juninho
3 Emerson
4 John Hendrie
5 Robbie Mustoe

IAN BAILEY
1 John Hickton
2 Willie Maddren
3 Graeme Souness
4 Emerson
5 Craig Johnston

LENNIE LAWRENCE
1 Wilf Mannion
2 George Hardwick
3 Graeme Souness
4 Gary Pallister
5 Craig Johnston

ARTHUR FITZSIMONS
1 Wilf Mannion
2 George Hardwick
3 Brian Clough
4 Jimmy Gordon
5 Dicky Robinson

JAN FJORTOFT
1 Graeme Souness
2 Gary Pallister
3 Fabrizio Ravanelli
4 Bryan Robson
5 Craig Johnston

SIMON COLEMAN
1 Gary Pallister
2 Tony Mowbray
3 Stephen Pears
4 Robbie Mustoe
5 Fabrizio Ravanelli

GIANLUCA FESTA
1 Fabrizio Ravanelli
2 Emerson
3 Juninho
4 Bryan Robson
5 Vladimir Kinder

ANDREW CAMPBELL
1 Juninho
2 Fabrizio Ravanelli
3 John Hendrie
4 Bernie Slaven
5 Emerson

KELHAM O'HANLON
1 Bobby Murdoch
2 Graeme Souness
3 Willie Maddren
4 David Armstrong
5 Kevin Beattie

ALAN FOGGON
1 Graeme Souness
2 Bobby Murdoch
3 Willie Maddren
4 John Hendrie
5 David Armstrong

MICK BURNS
1 Graeme Souness
2 David Armstrong
3 Craig Johnston
4 Bosko Jankovic
5 Willie Maddren

GRAEME HEDLEY
1 Graeme Souness
2 David Armstrong
3 Craig Johnston
4 Juninho
5 Terry Cooper

BRIAN LAWS
1 Graeme Souness
2 Craig Johnston
3 Tony Mowbray
4 Stephen Pears
5 Juninho

CHRIS MORRIS
1 Bryan Robson
2 Juninho
3 Graeme Souness
4 Gary Pallister
5 Nigel Pearson

MARK BURKE
1 Graeme Souness
2 Gary Pallister
3 Bryan Robson
4 Juninho
5 Colin Cooper

MY TOP 5
DAVID MILLS
1 John Hickton
2 Graeme Souness
3 Willie Maddren
4 Alan Peacock
5 Steve Pears

IAN JOHNSON
1 Bryan Robson
2 Bernie Slaven
3 Steve Pears
4 Tony Mowbray
5 Robbie Mustoe

ANDY TODD
1 Tony Mowbray
2 Gary Pallister
3 Stephen Pears
4 Bernie Slaven
5 Robbie Mustoe

PAUL KERR
1 Graeme Souness
2 Gary Hamilton
3 Juninho
4 Gary Pallister
5 Robbie Mustoe

HARRY BELL
1 Wilf Mannion
2 George Hardwick
3 Micky Fenton
4 Dicky Robinson
5 Jimmy Gordon

GEOFF WALKER
1 Wilf Mannion
2 George Hardwick
3 Brian Clough
4 Micky Fenton
5 Rolando Ugolini

DICKY ROOKS
1 Brian Clough
2 Alan Peacock
3George Hardwick
4 Gordon Jones
5 John Hickton

RAY YEOMAN
1 Brian Clough
2 Willie Fernie
3 Bill Harris
4 Alan Peacock
5 John Hickton

STAN ANDERSON
1 Wilf Mannion
2 Stuart Boam
3 John Hickton
4 John Craggs
5 Willie Maddren

JOHNNY SPUHLER
1 Alex McCrae
2 Dicky Robinson
3 George Hardwick
4 Wilf Mannion
5 Micky Fenton

RAY BILCLIFF
1 Wilf Mannion
2 Bill Harris
3 George Hardwick
4 Dicky Robinson
5 Brian Clough

PAUL KERR
1 Graeme Souness
2 Gary Hamilton
3 Juninho
4 Gary Pallister
5 Robbie Mustoe

TOMMY WRIGHT
1 Graeme Souness
2 Gary Pallister
3 Steve Pears
4 Gary Hamilton
5 John Hendrie

ANDREW CAMPBELL
1 Juninho
2 Fabrizio Ravanelli
3 John Hendrie
4 Bernie Slaven
5 Emerson

ALF WOOD
1 Graeme Souness
2 Willie Maddren
3 Bobby Murdoch
4 Jim Platt
5 Terry Cooper

GARY WALSH
1 Graeme Souness
2 Steve Pears
3 Brian Clough
4 Juninho
5 Gary Pallister

DARREN WOOD
1 Graeme Souness
2 Willie Maddren
3 David Armstrong
4 Mark Proctor
5 David Hodgson

ALAN MOORE
1 Bernie Slaven
2 John Hendrie
3 Robbie Mustoe
4 Curtis Fleming
5 Stuart Ripley

MICHAEL BARRON
1 Juninho
2 Tony Mowbray
3 Bernie Slaven
4 Stephen Pears
5 John Hendrie

PETER BEAGRIE
1 Heine Otto
2 Willie Maddren
3 David Mills
4 David Armstrong
5 Craig Johnston

COLIN ROSS
1 Bobby Murdoch
2 Graeme Souness
3 Willie Maddren
4 David Armstrong
5 John Hickton

DEAN GLOVER
1 Graeme Souness
2 Gary Pallister
3 Tony Mowbray
4 Bernie Slaven
5 Gary Hamilton

ALAN FOGGON
1 Graeme Souness
2 Bobby Murdoch
3 Willie Maddren
4 John Hendrie
5 David Armstrong

KEITH O'HALLORAN
1 Juninho
2 John Hendrie
3 Robbie Mustoe
4 Emerson
5 Curtis Fleming

PAT CUFF
1 Juninho
2 Graeme Souness
3 David Armstrong
4 Wilf Mannion
5 Brian Clough

PHIL STAMP
1 Juninho
2 Emerson
3 Gary Pallister
4 Fabrizio Ravanelli
5 John Hendrie

NEIL COX
1 Graeme Souness
2 Gary Pallister
3 Craig Johnston
4 Mark Proctor
5 Nick Barmby

DEREK WHYTE
1 Graeme Souness
2 Gary Pallister
3 Juninho
4 Emerson
5 Fabrizio Ravanelli

MARK SUMMERBELL
1 Juninho
2 Emerson
3 Gary Pallister
4 Bernie Slaven
5 Steven Pears

MY TOP 5
NIGEL PEARSON
1 Graeme Souness
2 Juninho
3 David Armsrtong
4 Emerson
5 John Hendrie

Part Two

BEST *of the rest:*

A further twenty five players who received votes from their peers

David Mills (1969-78, 84-86)

Born: Whitby, 06-12-51.

Fleet-footed forward David Mills provided loyal service to Boro for a decade before shattering the club's and Britain's transfer records by becoming the country's first half-million pound footballer. Though he never scored as many goals as he possibly should, Mills was an exciting player who made more than 350 appearances for the club in two spells.

Mills joined Boro in July 1968. Stan Anderson gave him his debut as a 17-year-old substitute in the last game of the 1968/69 season against Birmingham. His first start came at the back-end of the next term when he crowned his full debut with a goal against Swindon. Mills had to wait patiently before fully establishing himself in the side but he was crucial in Boro's promotion season of 1973/74 under Jack Charlton.

His form brought him to the attention of the England under-23 selectors and in 1976 Jack Charlton reportedly turned down a £200,000 offer from Liverpool. But three years later, Boro agreed to sell Mills to West Brom. Despite the huge fee, chances were limited at the Hawthorns and he was sold for just £30,000 to Sheffield Wednesday in 1983 and then on to Newcastle. The following year, Willie Maddren brought Mills back to Ayresome Park on a free transfer. He finished top scorer in 1984/85 but injury ruled him out throughout his final season with the club.

Bosco Jankovic (1979-81)

Born: Sarajevo, 22-05-51.

When Bosco Jankovic ran out for his Boro debut in 1979 he slipped as he crossed the line to enter the fray as a substitute. Fortunately, the Yugoslav proved to be adept with the ball at his feet and was an exciting addition to the Boro side. John Neal signed the international from Yugoslav team Zeljeznicar in February 1979. After his debut as a substitute against Bristol City, a first start followed at Bolton and he scored his first goal in a 3-1 win at Derby. In the next two seasons, Jankovic showed his talent, providing the team with width and also playing in the centre of the forward line. His most successful season came in 1980/81 when he finished as top scorer with 12 goals from just 21 starts.

When John Neal left at the end of the season, however, Jankovic was released to return to Yugoslavia with Boro holding on to his registration. Neal, by then manager of Chelsea, attempted to re-sign Jankovic soon after but his bid failed and he remained in Yugoslavia. Sadly Jankovic died in 1994, aged just 43.

Irving Nattrass (1979-86)

Born: Fishburn, 12-12-52.

After becoming Boro's record signing in 1979, Irving Nattrass suffered a nightmare string of injuries but he went on to become a good club servant, playing in nine different positions in his seven years at Ayresome Park. Nattrass started his career at Newcastle, becoming a professional in July 1970. The high point of his career for the Magpies came when he played in the 1976 League Cup final and won an England under-23 cap. But he was robbed of further games by injury and also missed out on the possibility of full caps when he was tipped for a call-up.

When Newcastle were relegated in 1979, Nattrass was keen to stay in the top flight and it was Boro manager John Neal who persuaded him to make the move down to Middlesbrough. A tribunal was required to set the fee of £475,000 - a Boro record that lasted nine years until the arrival of Peter Davenport.

An Achilles injury delayed Nattrass's debut for a month and he also suffered three hairline fractures in his leg in his first season. But over the coming years, Nattrass established himself as a reliable and versatile performer for the club.

Stephen Bell (1981-85)

Born: Middlesbrough, 13-03-65.

When highly talented winger Stephen Bell made his Boro debut aged a mere 16 in January 1982, he was earmarked for a very bright future. But by the age of 20, Bell's career had all but ended in disappointment. After his debut against Southampton, Bell had to wait until the start of the following season for another chance. But throughout 1982/83, Bell, by now 17, was ever-present. Bobby Murdoch and then Malcolm Allison had faith in their young prodigy who was fast developing into a star. As well as his skilful running, Bell could also weigh in with his share of goals, finishing as second top scorer in 82/83.

Ultimately, this was to prove the peak of Bell's career. After less than 100 appearances for the club, Bell's contract was cancelled in 1985 while Willie Maddren was manager. He drifted out of the professional game before being given a chance to resurrect his career at Portsmouth by Alan Ball. But Bell walked out on Pompey and returned to the north-east. His last games at league level were for Darlington where he played 40 games.

David Mills, pictured scoring against Peter Shilton.

Irving Nattrass was a record signing for Boro in 1979.

Bosco Jankovic was one of Boro's first overseas stars.

Teenage sensation Stephen Bell.

Billy Pease (1926-33)

Born: Leeds, 30-09-1898.

Pre-war favourite Billy Pease was a pacy winger with a definite eye for goal. His goals were a major contribution to two promotions in the late 1920's. Pease started his career with Leeds City after the First World War but when the club was expelled from the league in 1919, he moved to Northampton Town as they secured a place in Division Three South.

Boro paid £2,000 for his services in May 1926 and Pease made his debut in a 3-0 defeat against Chelsea in the first game of the 1926/27 season. The term ended in promotion into Division One with Pease finishing as second highest scorer behind George Camsell's phenomenal 59 goals. Relegation followed but Pease was a virtual ever-present, scoring almost a goal a game as Boro bounced back as champions of Division Two. He continued playing a vital role for the club before losing his place in the 1932/33 campaign.

Pease's one England cap came early in his Boro career. He played in a 3-3 draw with Wales in February 1927. He left Boro for £500 to join Luton Town in June 1933. He died in 1955.

Frank Spraggon (1963-76)

Born: Marley Hill, 27-10-45.

Defender Frank Spraggon had to wait five years before establishing himself in the Middlesbrough side but he went on to become a loyal club servant who always gave 100 per cent. He joined Boro in 1962 and made his debut in a league cup tie against Bradford in October 1963. Over the coming seasons, Spraggon spent most of his time in the reserves, making just a handful of appearances as Boro dropped into the Third Division. Spraggon won a firm place once Boro had regained their place in Division Two. His first goal took a while in coming and it was in a 4-2 win over Birmingham in late 1969 that he first found the net.

Spraggon spent a spell out of the side in the 1971/72 campaign when a cartilage operation and then problems with blurred vision forced him out for seven months. He was granted a testimonial in 1975 when Boro took on Dinamo Zagreb at Ayresome Park. After being released by Boro, Spraggon spent the summer of 1976 playing for Minnesota Kicks in the USA and played one game for Hartlepool before a knee injury forced him to retire. He currently works for the MFC Football Academy.

Eddie Holliday (1957-62, 1965-66)

Born: Barnsley, 17-06-39.

As Boro piled on the goals in the late 1950s through the likes of Brian Clough and Alan Peacock, the accurate crossing and speedy wing play of Eddie Holliday brought on much of the success for his team-mates in the penalty box. After progressing through the junior ranks, 18-year-old Holliday came into the Boro side for a visit to West Ham in December 1957. He was picked for the England under-23 side to play Hungary in September 1959 and was swiftly promoted to the full England side, making his debut alongside Clough, who was also making his first appearance, against Wales in October. Two more caps swiftly followed but in 1960, Holliday was back with the under-23s never to play for the full side again.

In March 1962, Bob Dennison agreed to Holliday's transfer to First Division Sheffield Wednesday. Unfortunately for Holliday, opportunities were infrequent at Hillsborough and in the summer of 1965 he was back to Ayresome Park. The move failed to rekindle former glories, however, and when Boro were relegated to Division Three at the end of the season, Holliday joined Southern League Hereford. Workington gave him the chance to resurrect his league career in February 1968 and a spell followed at Peterborough. But in 1970, Holliday broke his leg and was forced to retire.

Stan Anderson (1965-66)

Born: Horden, 27-02-34.

The man who was to manage Boro for seven years, remains the only player to have captained all three of the North-east's top teams. Although his playing days at Boro were short, he was a stylish midfielder who was an excellent leader of men. Anderson started his career at Sunderland after being turned down by Boro. In 10 years at Roker Park, Anderson notched up more than 400 appearances for the club and came to the attention of first the England under-23 and then the full England selectors.

Newcastle paid £30,000 for Anderson in November 1963 and, as skipper, he led the club to the Second Division title in his first full season. But in November 1965, he was on the move again, accepting Raich Carter's offer to become Boro's first ever player-coach, making a goal-scoring debut against Cardiff.

Five months later, Anderson accepted the chance of becoming Boro's manager and hung up his boots. Relegation to the Third Division followed but he steered the club back into Division Two at the first attempt. Despite continually being placed in the upper reaches of the Second Division, Anderson failed to take his team into the top flight and resigned in January 1973. His team were renowned as a good footballing side and Jack Charlton took his players, with minimal changes, into Division One a year later. Management spells came later at AEK Athens and Panathinaikos in Greece and also Doncaster and Bolton.

England international Eddie Holliday displays his ball skills.

Frank Spraggon was a vital member of Boro's promotion side of 1973/74.

Winger Billy Pease could make and take goals.

David Chadwick (1966-70)

Born: Ooctamund, India, 19-08-43.

Winger David Chadwick was plucked from Southampton's reserves to help Boro out of the Third Division at the first attempt. His tricky runs and ability to hold on to the ball were crucial in helping the club out of the lowest position it had ever slipped to.

Southampton had given Chadwick just 25 starts in six years when Stan Anderson made him one of his first signings in July 1966. He made the long journey north and his debut came in the opening game of the 1966/67 season in a 3-2 win over Colchester. He was a regular as Boro won promotion and then in the first campaign back in Division Two but missed out for much of the 1968/69 season and was eventually sold to Halifax in January 1970.

After almost 100 games for Halifax, Chadwick returned to the South Coast to join Bournemouth. A loan spell at Torquay followed before he ended his playing days with Gillingham.

Willie Whigham (1966-72)

Born: Airdrie, 09-10-39.

Cult favourite Willie Whigham was renowned for his erratic displays in the Boro goal. At times brilliant, he was also prone to errors and was occasionally rebellious off the field but is one of the club's best remembered keepers. In Scotland, Whigham had been Falkirk's number one when the club was promoted from the First Division in 1961 and came to the attention of Boro boss Stan Anderson. A fee of £10,000 brought Whigham onto Ayresome Park in October 1966 and he replaced Des McPartland to come in for a debut against Watford. Boro lost the game 2-0 but went to secure promotion to Division Two with Whigham being credited with a number of match-winning displays.

The Scot missed several games while in a contract dispute with the club and put in a transfer request in 1969/70 but returned as an ever-present for the following campaign. A 4-1 derby defeat against Sunderland a year later, however, prompted the selection of young understudy Jim Platt and Whigham never regained his place. He returned to Scotland to play for Dumbarton before reverting to the North-east in 1974 to play a handful of games for Darlington. Although he now lives in Scotland, he still regularly returns to Teesside to watch Boro.

Bill Linacre (1949-52)

Born: Chesterfield, 10-08-24.

But for a broken leg, Bill Linacre could have become an excellent member of Boro's post-war side. The talented winger was jinxed with injury, breaking his leg three times in his career, but was an impressive performer in his 35 games for the club. Linacre's first two leg breaks came in a luckless season for his first club, Chesterfield. But he made full recoveries to earn a move to Manchester City in 1947. Two years on, David Jack paid £18,000 to take Linacre to Ayresome Park and he made his debut against Charlton in September 1949.

His devastating leg break came on his return to Maine Road in February 1950. The injury forced Linacre to sit out the rest of the season and he struggled to regain his place, having to wait more than year before his next game. After starting the 1951/52 season, Linacre once again lost his place and dropped out of the league to play for Goole Town.

Hartlepool gave Linacre the chance to resurrect his career and he played 89 times in three seasons at the club. His last move saw him return to Derbyshire to play for Mansfield Town though he later played for Blyth Spartans.

Ian Baird (1990-91)

Born: Rotherham, 01-04-64.

Nomadic striker Ian Baird became known as 'big, bad Bairdy' in his short spell with Middlesbrough. His one full season at the club brought him the player of the year award after enjoying one of the most prolific spells of his career at the start of the 1990/91 season.

A Southampton apprentice, Baird spent his early days on loan to Cardiff, where he scored six in 12 games, and then Newcastle. He left the Saints in 1985 to join Leeds for £75,000. In three seasons at Elland Road, Baird found the net 33 times in 90 games and Portsmouth stepped in with a £285,000 bid to take Baird back to the South Coast. Seven months and 20 games later, Baird was heading back up to Elland Road when Leeds snatched him back for a cut-price £120,000. Two years on, Boro boss Bruce Rioch paid £500,000 to add Baird to his forward line.

Baird made his debut in February 1990 against his old club Portsmouth. In the following season, he finished second top scorer behind Bernie Slaven as Boro reached the Second Division play-offs but in the close season he moved on to join Hearts for £300,000. A spell at Bristol City followed before Baird joined Brighton as they struggled to maintain their league status in the 1996/97 season.

Willie Whigham Boro's unorthodox keeper.

Winger Dave Chadwick impressed for Boro.

Ian Baird's all-action displays were appreciated by his team-mates.

Winger Billy Linacre's career was beset with injury problems.

Gianluca Festa (1997-)

Born: Cagliari, 15-03-69.

Powerful centre-half Gianluca Festa became Bryan Robson's second Italian signing when he followed the path of Fabrizio Ravanelli from Italy to Teesside. The Sardinian-born defender started his career at hometown club Cagliari and, after a spell on loan at regional league side Fesulcis, helped the club in its miraculous rise from Serie C into Serie A and the UEFA Cup. He was chased by most of the country's top clubs but elected to join Inter Milan in 1993. He was once again loaned out - this time to Roma - before becoming a regular at the San Siro.

After two seasons as a consistent performer in the centre of defence, Festa found himself out of favour at Inter and was once again attracting interest from other clubs. But it was abroad that Festa saw his future and elected to move to the Cellnet Riverside Stadium in a £2.7 million deal having earlier played at the stadium in a pre-season game for Inter.

Festa made his debut against Sheffield Wednesday in January 1997 when he scored in a 4-2 win, and immediately slotted into the Boro defence, winning plaudits for his commanding and strong displays as Bor made great progress in both cup competitions.

Ralph Birkett (1935-38)

Born: Ashford, 09-01-13.

Pacy winger Ralph Birkett made an immediate impact on his arrival at Boro in 1935, scoring four goals in seven games to help the club stave off relegation from the top flight. He went on to become a star of the excellent pre-war Boro side. Birkett joined Boro from Arsenal for £5,900 in March 1935. He had struggled for opportunities at the all-star Arsenal, playing just 19 games in his two years at Highbury. Arsenal had paid £2,000 to take Birkett from Torquay in 1933 but agreed to allow him to move to Ayresome Park.

He made his debut against Preston in March 1935 and scored twice in his first home game a week later. After being left out for three games in the run-in, including an 8-0 thrashing at the hands of his old club Arsenal, Birkett returned with another brace as Boro stayed in Division One. He was second top scorer for the next campaign and was called up by England to play Ireland in October 1935.

He became a popular figure among the Boro supporters and there was dismay when he was sold to rivals Newcastle for £6,000 in July 1938. A year later, war brought a premature end to Birkett's career. He now lives on the South Coast but returned to Teesside for the last ever match at Ayresome Park.

Derrick Downing (1965-72)

Born: Doncaster, 03-11-45.

Derrick Downing was a successful forward with Boro, renowned for his brave diving headers and long throws into the penalty box. He passed the 200-mark for Boro in a seven-year spell which included promotion from the Third Division. He had made his Boro debut at Plymouth in September 1965, having earlier played for Frickley Colliery. His first season ended in relegation but Downing won a regular slot a month into the 1966/67 season and helped secure promotion. The next campaign was mostly watched from the sidelines but Downing bounced back to become a familiar sight for Boro fans.

In May 1972 Stan Anderson decided Downing was not part of his plans and he moved to Orient. A century of appearances followed at Brisbane Road before Downing moved to York City and later back to the North-east for a spell at Hartlepool.

Mick Kennedy (1982-84)

Born: Salford, 09-04-61.

Aggressive midfielder Kennedy won friends in the crowd with his uncompromising style but was not so popular with referees, earning a poor disciplinary record throughout his career. After starting his career with Halifax, Kennedy established himself at Huddersfield following a £10,000 move. Two years later, after being named as the Terriers' player of the year for 1981/82, Kennedy made a £100,000 switch to Middlesbrough.

He came in for his Boro debut against Sheffield Wednesday in August 1982 and it was only a month later that Kennedy was sent off against Grimsby. After two seasons as a regular in the midfield, his hard-working, tough displays won admirers but a second sending-off against Brighton in May 1984 proved to be Kennedy's penultimate game and he was transferred to Portsmouth, once again for £100,000.

Two international caps for Ireland followed at Fratton Park in his three years with Pompey - the longest time Kennedy spent with any club. Mid-way through the 1987/88 season, he moved on to Bradford before enjoying spells with Leicester and Luton and ending his career with Stoke.

Gianluca Festa scored on his Boro debut against Sheffield Wednesday.

Ralph Birkett climbs on board the Boro coach outside Ayresome Park.

Derrick Downing was renowned for his diving headers during his time at Boro.

Nigel Pearson (1994-)

Born: Nottingham, 21-08-63.

Inspirational Boro captain Nigel Pearson has been a commanding centre-back throughout his playing career, leading by example. Though injuries have played their part, he has been a key player in bringing success to each of his clubs including promotion to the Premier League in his first season with Boro.

Shrewsbury Town brought Pearson into the league, signing the tall centre-half from Heanor Town. He stepped effectively into the Shrews side before a serious injury suffered in 1984 kept him out for more than 12 months. He returned to become a vital part of the Shrews Second Division team and earned a move to Sheffield Wednesday after impressing when the two sides met in a League Cup tie.

He moved to Hillsborough in 1987 and, after relegation in 1990, skippered the side to a historic victory over Manchester United in the League Cup final of 1991 and promotion back to the top flight at the first attempt, scoring 12 goals in the process. Injuries caused Pearson to miss games including the 1994 League Cup and FA Cup finals - but Bryan Robson made him one of his first signings on taking over at Boro. Since the move, he has been a rock at the back for the club and a respected captain though a neck injury forced him to miss a large chunk of the 1996/97 campaign.

Lindy Delapenha (1949-58)

Born: Kingston, Jamaica, 20-05-27.

West Indian-born Lindy Delapenha combined pace and power to provide the punch in Boro's post-war front-line. Playing either on the wing or at inside-forward he was leading scorer for three seasons and made up for his lack of height with a robust presence in opposition penalty boxes. After serving with the RAF in the war, Delapenha had joined Arsenal as an amateur and then moved on to Portsmouth. After just seven games for Pompey, he was signed by Boro manager David Jack in April 1950.

Delapenha made his debut against Fulham in the last game of the 1949/50 season and played almost every game as Boro finished sixth in Division One the following term. For the four subsequent seasons, Delapenha was the club's most consistent goalscorer and established a reputation as a clinical penalty taker. In the late 1950's Delapenha's mantle as top goalscorer was taken on by the prolific Brian Clough and in June 1958 he was sold to Third Division Mansfield. He went on to play more than 100 games for the Stags over three seasons, scoring 27 goals before ending his professional career and later returning to his native Jamaica.

Bill Gates (1961-74)

Born: Ferryhill, 08-05-44.

Gates broke into the Boro team as a teenager and went on to loyally serve the club for 13 years. Playing most of his games at centre-back, Gates was rarely seen as an automatic choice but was a popular and hard-working club man. Gates' debut came against Luton in September 1961 just after his 17th birthday as a replacement for regular centre-half Ken Thomson. He began to win a more regular slot after the departure of Cyril Knowles in 1964 and netted his first goal against Scunthorpe in January 1967.

Gates never managed a season as an ever-present - his best campaign coming in the 1970/71 term - but notched up more than 300 games. He suffered a fractured jaw in a game against Manchester United in 1969 but showed his fighting spirit by playing on. In May 1974, more than 30,000 Boro supporters turned out for a testimonial match with league champions Leeds but two months later, Gates was released by the club. After selling up his successful sports retail business, he now lives in Cayman Islands.

Vladimir Kinder (1996-)

Born: Bratislava, 09-03-69.

Not too many players have the honour of being named their country's player of the year for three years running, but Vladimir Kinder has marked himself out as a star from the relatively new country of Slovakia. Kinder was spotted playing for top Slovakian side Slovan Bratislava. He joined his hometown club as a schoolboy and established himself as a regular at left-back. He helped the club to earn three consecutive Slovakian league titles and was a regular in European competition.

More than 20 international caps had followed by the time he moved to Boro in a £1.3 million deal. He had earlier come across to Teesside for a trial and impressed in a reserve game. Kinder made his Boro debut in an FA Cup tie with non-league Hednesford Town and showed his ability to play the ball with both feet and defend strongly. He scored his first goal for the club in a 6-1 win over Derby in March 1997.

Arthur Kaye (1960-65)

Born: Barnsley, 09-05-33.

Arthur Kaye may not have been the tallest of Boro players at just 5ft 3in tall, but he made up for his lack of height with his skill on the ball on the wing for Boro in the early 1960's. The former England schoolboy joined Barnsley on his 17th birthday and made a big impact with his performances on the right flank for his hometown club. In eight years at Barnsley, Kaye clocked up more than 250 games for the Terriers and was capped at England under-23 level and played for the Football League representative side.

Blackpool signed Kaye in May 1959 and he was earmarked as a replacement for Stanley Matthews. But as the legendary winger exceeded all expectations by extending his playing career, chances were limited at Blackpool and Kaye switched to Boro in a £10,000 deal. He made his debut against Lincoln in November 1960, quickly establishing himself in the Boro side and weighing in with his fair share of goals. After five years at Ayresome Park, he made the final move of his career, joining Colchester.

Lindy Delapenha displays his shooting prowess.

Nigel Pearson, an inspirational captain.

Vladimir Kinder made a quick impact at the Riverside.

Tough tackling Bill Gates dispossesses George Best in a 1970's cup tie.

Steve Vickers (1993-)

Born: Bishop Auckland, 13-10-67.

Boro' s player of the year for the 1995/96 season has been praised for his calm, composed defending since the club rose into the Premier League. But Vickers had to wait until he had reached the age of 27 before he completed the rise from Northern League to Premiership. Tranmere Rovers signed him from Spennymoor in 1985 after he had turned down Boro. He went on to make almost 400 league and cup appearances for Tranmere as the Wirral club rose from the old Fourth Division to become perennial play-off candidates in Division One. Lennie Lawrence elected to bring Vickers back to the North-east in December 1993. The Boro manager was under pressure to buy a striker at the time but rightly predicted that his £700,000 buy would be a good club servant.

Vickers started his Boro career as a substitute at Bristol City and established a regular place, replacing Nicky Mohan, before the end of the season. Vickers was a vital member of the team that won promotion to the top flight in Bryan Robson's first season at the club and, once in the Premier League, won admiration from Robson for his intelligent defending.

Terry Cochrane (1978-83)

Born: Killyleagh, 23-01-53.

Talented wing-man Terry Cochrane was a thorn in the side of many an opposition full-back while occupying the right flank for Boro. He became the club's record signing when he joined Boro in 1978. As a youngster, trials at Everton and Nottingham Forest had failed to win Cochrane a contract and he had played for Linfield, Coleraine and Derry City in the Irish League. He was called up for Northern Ireland for his first cap while still with Coleraine and his chance in England was eventually provided by Burnley who paid £38,000 for his services in October 1976.

Boro manager John Neal was impressed enough with the tricky winger to splash out a club record £238,000. He went straight into the Boro side, making his first start against Manchester United at Old Trafford in October 1978. Neal rated Cochrane as one of the best wingers in the league but chances were fewer under Malcolm Allison and in 1983, Cochrane moved on to Gillingham, where he topped 100 games before spells with Millwall, Hartlepool and Dallas in the North American Soccer League. Whilst with Boro, he won many caps for Northern Ireland and once scored against England at Wembley.

Ray Yeoman (1958-63)

Born: Perth, 13-05-34.

Boro boss Bob Dennison was a big fan of Scotsman Ray Yeoman, signing him twice in his managerial career. Though Dennison had to wait four years after joining Boro before he could tempt Yeoman from his former club, Northampton Town, he went on to have a fine career at Ayresome Park.

Dennison first signed Yeoman for Northampton in 1953. He had been spotted playing for St Johnstone. A year later, Dennison left to go to Boro and Yeoman went on to play more than 150 games for the Cobblers, playing mostly at wing-half.

In November 1958, Yeoman made the switch to Ayresome Park for a fee of £3,750. He made his debut in a 2-0 defeat away to Sheffield Wednesday a month later and immediately started a run of consecutive games that would include four full seasons. The next game in which Yeoman was missing from the Boro line-up was for the opening game of the 1963/64 season - 207 league and cup games and almost five years after his debut.

In June 1964, Yeoman left Boro to move to Darlington. Joining as a 30-year-old, he played more than 100 games at Feethams and became the Quakers' manager in 1968. After a two-year spell in charge, he left and became youth team manager at Sunderland.

Darren Wood (1981-85)

Born: Scarborough, 09-06-64.

Darren Wood was a stylish defender who was a key young player for Boro after coming through the youth ranks. After impressing at a young age he was reluctantly sold, only for his career to end in his mid-20s through injury. After turning professional in July 1981, Wood made his debut at the age of 17 against Southampton in September of that year. Despite his young age, Wood had established a regular slot by the end of the season under Bobby Murdoch. He held on to his place following the arrival of Malcolm Allison in October 1982 and was one of only two ever-presents in the 1982/83 season and repeated the feat for the following campaign.

But early in the 1984/85 season, Boro reluctantly agreed to sell the young star to Chelsea. Former Boro manager John Neal snapped up the player he had seen as a junior at the club and took him to Stamford Bridge. In four seasons at the London club, Wood enjoyed a successful career, playing more than 100 times for the Blues. In January 1989, he moved on to Sheffield Wednesday where he played alongside Nigel Pearson and Mark Proctor. But Wood played only 11 times for the Owls and was forced to retire with a back injury.

Tricky winger Terry Cochrane in his Boro hey-day.

Ray Yeoman was a consistent Boro performer.

Darren Wood was seen as a star of the future during his time at Ayresome Park.

Steve Vickers' fine form made him a fixture in the Boro defence.

Part Three

The Fans' Rating

A message to all Boro fans from Juninho

It makes me feel very proud to be honoured by the Middlesbrough supporters in this way. They are the best I've ever come across, either in Brazil or England.

When I run on to the pitch before every match, it is great to hear them cheering and shouting my name regardless of whether the team is winning or losing.

It is very important for all the players that the supporters always encourage the team, as it gives us the confidence to play well.

Over the years there have been many great players who have appeared for Middlesbrough, like Wilf Mannion, who I have met, and it is amazing to think that after less than two seasons on Teesside, the supporters have such a high regard for me.

I would like to take this opportunity to thank all the fans for their loyal support while I've been at Middlesbrough and I assure them that I will be doing everything in my power to bring them success in the future.

Best Wishes,

The Fans' Top 50

The top Boro stars of all-time, as chosen by the club's supporters.

1	JUNINHO
2	Bernie SLAVEN
3	Wilf MANNION
4	Graeme SOUNESS
5	John HICKTON
6	John HENDRIE
7	Brian CLOUGH
8	Tony MOWBRAY
9	EMERSON
10	Willie MADDREN
11	Fabrizio RAVANELLI
12	George HARDWICK
13	Stephen PEARS
14	George CAMSELL
15	Gary PALLISTER
16	Curtis FLEMING
17	David ARMSTRONG
18	Craig HIGNETT
19	Robbie MUSTOE
20	Bobby MURDOCH
21	Craig JOHNSTON
22	Nick BARMBY
23	Stuart BOAM
24	Dave HODGSON
25	Bryan ROBSON
26	Uwe FUCHS
27	Heine OTTO
28	Stuart RIPLEY
29	Mikkel BECK
30	David MILLS
31	Bill HARRIS
32	Tim WILLIAMSON
33	Jim PLATT
34	Terry COCHRANE
35	John O'ROURKE
36	Alan FOGGON
37	Micky FENTON
38	Paul WILKINSON
39	Jan FJORTOFT
40	John CRAGGS
41	Gianluca FESTA
42	Eddie HOLLIDAY
43	Lindy DELAPENHA
44	Cyril KNOWLES
45	Hugh McILMOYLE
46	Bob BAXTER
47	Gordon JONES
48	Colin COOPER
49	Steve VICKERS
50	Terry COOPER

A selection of quotes about the fans' favourites

"**Wilf Mannion** was poetry in motion. He had brilliant footwork, a marvellous shimmy, could out-jump the best, made them and scored them. He could beat a defence without even touching the ball. He was the greatest - who am I to disagree with Matthews, Lawton and the rest who thought so too. Oh, for just a sight of him again!"
Mr H. Graham, Middlesbrough.

"For his all-round ability on a football field and his attitude towards the best game in the world, I pick ***Bryan Robson****. If every footballer had his determination and will to win, we'd never have any losers. He's not only the best footballer I have seen in a Boro shirt, he's the best thing that has ever happened to Boro in my 50 years of life. You can see his style and commitment to the game coming out in players like Mustoe, Fleming, Moore, Stamp, Hignett and a lot of the young reserves. I hope he never leaves."*
Colin James Hinds, Brotton.

"Apart from **Juninho's** obvious skill, it is his commitment to the club that is really impressive. It is noticeable that even if things don't come off, he goes on trying. For a little guy from Brazil, he is a real battler."
Harry Pearson, Riverside Roar columnist and author.

"There can only be one number one - **John Hickton** - my boyhood hero and a true Boro star who would have gained more national recognition if he had played all of his Boro career in the top flight. I saw him make his debut against Workington in Division Three and followed the big fella's career until he retired, seeing most of his Boro goals in that time. I still feel like saying "We're not worthy" even when I meet him today."
Mark Page, MFC, PA announcer and DJ.

"Not only did **Brian Clough** score consistently for Boro, with feet and head, but in my opinion he has been the best striker in English football since the war - better than Greaves, Law, Lineker, Best, Shearer, etc. Just take a look at his goalscoring record."
Mr F. Gregg, Barnsley.

Three of Boro's Best (from left): Robbie Mustoe, Nick Barmby and Juninho.

Champions! Boro's best ever 'keeper Stephen Pears (left) celebrates the 1995 First Division championship with skipper Nigel Pearson. This picture was taken in the Ayresome Park dressing room on the night of Pears' testimonial match against Manchester United.

MY TOP 5
Michael Brown
Shildon

1. Stephen Pears
2. John Hendrie
3. Bernie Slaven
4. Tony Mowbray
5. Juninho

"Since my first Boro match in 1988 I have witnessed many great saves from **Stephen Pears**. Many of Pearsy's performances helped Boro win games by a single goal and in the long run were crucial in helping us win promotion or avoid relegation. He was a Boro hero who was cruelly denied the chance to prove himself at international level."

John Matthew Innes, Middleton St George, Darlington.

"Being a defender myself, it's easy to see why I selected **Gary Pallister** as my favourite player. His partnership with "Mogga" was widely recognised as one of the best central defensive partnerships in the league and that is great credit to the lad who came from non-league.

"Pally had tremendous pace but also brought the ball out of defence with great ease, often turning defence into attack. His achievements with Manchester United and England make Pally one of Boro's favourite sons, and rightly so. I met Gary many times off the pitch, once in a night-club when I asked him who he thought would win the Premiership that year. He said Arsenal, only for Man United to win the championship for the first time in 26 years."

Michael Norman, Stockton.

*"**John Hickton** was such an exciting player. He was like a Wild West gunslinger when he faced the keeper for a penalty. His run-up was tremendous, it started in Stockton and by the time he reached the penalty spot he was unstoppable."*
Robert Nichols, editor of Boro fanzine Fly Me To The Moon.

"**Brian Clough** was our most prolific goalscorer and after his playing days he was a great ambassador for the game."
Jason Allen, Guisborough.

Pre-war goalkeeping hero Dave Cumming was a big crowd pleaser.

"My best memory of **Wilf Mannion** is when he scored one of the goals against Charlton in 1950. He gathered the ball on the half-way line and went for goal. As Wilf put the ball in the net past Sam Bartram, his trailing foot touched Bartram's head, who tried to claim he had been fouled! Boro won 7-3."
Alan Clough, Billingham.

"**Juninho's** a gem. He has tremendous skill and talent and his knowledge of the game is remarkable. As the saying goes 'you don't get a diamond the size of a brick'!"
Lucy Raybould, Ingleby Barwick.

*"The reason for choosing **Wilf Mannion** as number one, if not for anything else, was his performance against Blackpool in 1947. Nevertheless he is still the best player the Boro have had play for them. I can remember the roar of excitement from the crowd when Wilf received the ball even when he was in the Boro half of the field. The Boro supporters felt something positive would happen. He was, after all, a true two-footed player and I just wish he could play for Boro in the Premiership."*
Mr J. M. Jackson, Marton.

"To have a player of **Juninho's** class playing for the Boro is unbelievable. He has never criticised the club or the area and always gives 110 per cent. In the history of MFC, he will go down as a legend."
Gary Knaggs, Norton.

German striker Uwe Fuchs may only have played 15 games in a Boro shirt but he became a cult hero in the Holgate End during 1994/95.

"When I was a boy, my father took me to see a great footballer called **Jackie Carr**. When I was older I went to see another footballer by the name of **George Camsell** who turned out to be Boro's best ever goal-scoring machine. His 59 goals was only to be beaten by another great goal scorer by the name of Dixie Dean with 60 goals for Everton. Both records have never been broken.

"Camsell had a number of games for England, scoring in all games he played. If not for Dixie Dean, Camsell would have had more caps which was harder in those day for a northerner. In those pre-war days and for 10 years after the war, a cap for England equals about 20 caps today.

"It was realised that Camsell would have been greater known but he refused to leave his favourite north of England to play with the likes of Bob Bastin and Alec James of the then great Arsenal."
William Moncur, Stockton.

"**Uwe Fuchs'** goals were vital in gaining Boro promotion to the Premiership in 1995. His goal ratio was first class considering that he was only here for less than four months. Yes, Uwe's goals, character and sheer determination will stick in my mind forever."
Michael Stone, Thornaby.

"**Juninho** is absolutely fabulous, the best player I've seen in a red shirt in over 40 years."
Mr S. McCulloch, Middlesbrough.

"At the time I was watching Boro, **John Hickton** personified the team. He had the dash, the barn-storming performances and also the ability to cock up as well! You look back to the 70's with rose-coloured spectacles but he was everything I would want in a goalscoring centre-forward."
Andrew Shields, Sports editor Time Out.

"**Bernie Slaven** was a finisher of style and class, a king. But because of his background and being unemployed for so long, he understood the hopes and aspirations of the common fan."
Alan Bell, Stockton.

*"**John Hickton** came at a real crisis time in the old Division Three. As a centre-half, he took charge from his first game, against Workington. As a striker, he was even better. Most of all, he was committed and loyal to Boro."*
George Littler, Hartburn.

"**Juninho** is such a delight to watch and his skills are exquisite. I also love his wonderful smile. What a player to have in a Boro shirt."
John Davies, Eston.

"My number one choice is **Wilf Mannion** for the brilliant and marvellous game he played against Blackpool at Ayresome Park. I would also pick Tim Williamson who I used to see when I was between 13 and 14 years old, then George Elliott, Brian Clough and Dicky Robinson, who I thought should have had an England cap."
George William Evans, Stockton.

Crowd favourite: Italian centre-back Gianluca Festa, pictured in action in the FA Cup win over Hednesford, made an immediate impact following his transfer from Inter Milan in 1997.

MY TOP 5
Andrew Morgan
Kirklevington

1 Juninho
2 Nigel Pearson
3 Robbie Mustoe
4 Fabrizio Ravanelli
5 Emerson

"**Tony Mowbray** epitomised everything about being a local boy who cared for his club during our troubled years with his leadership qualities and never-say-die attitude."
Andrew Richards, Redcar.

*"**Souness** was a stinging striker of the ball, had a tigerish tackle, was a superb passer ... and he lived in Chipchase Road!"*
Andy Smith, London.

"**Mannion** had all-round ability at football including balance, ball control, passing, vision, shooting, heading even the heavy leather footballs in use and getting international caps with England and Great Britain. If Ravanelli is worth £7 million, Mannion would be worth £70 million."
Jim McLaren, Middlesbrough.

"**Juninho's** skill and agility are breath-taking. He has all the skill but he is also fearless. So many teams try to put him out of the game but most fail, despite the over-the-top tackling he endures. He simply gets back up and gets on with the game. Amazing."
Bernadette Rizzi-Allan, Linthorpe.

"**John Hickton** was totally committed, totally consistent, totally dedicated. He never ceased trying, either going forward or tackling back. From the mid-60's to the mid-70's the only thing that changed about him was his hairstyle. It was wonderful to see his head go down in that peculiar running style of his because you knew he was off. There may have been better goalscorers than Hicky, more skilfully gifted than Hicky - but for me he epitomised the phrase 'a team player'."
Derek Field, Middlesbrough.

"**Wilf Mannion** just seemed to drift past people and it seemed to be so effortless. And not only was he a constructive player but he could put the ball in the back of the net and also jump twice his height."
Alan Keen M.P.

*"**Willie Maddren** was locally-born and our best ever defender. He always gave 100 per cent, was very quick and never dirty. He tackled strongly, covered brilliantly and was dominant in the air."*
John Severs, Durham City.

Gary Walsh, who picked up several votes from fans, celebrates the 3-1 Coca-Cola Cup victory over Newcastle United in November 1996.

The legendary Brian Clough scores one of over 200 Boro goals that made him one of the fans' favourites.

"To lift 30,000 fans sometimes takes genius, sometimes 100 per cent effort or just the fact that a certain player will be playing that day. To have a player in **Juninho** who does all these things and is a great ambassador for the club he loves, all over the world, is very very special."
Alan Johnson, Spennymoor.

"In my opinion, ***Hughie McIlmoyle*** *was the most complete footballer I have actually seen play for the Boro. Not only was he the best header of the ball, he was equally gifted on the ground."*
Malcolm Stewart, Ingleby Barwick.

"Not only did **Wilf Mannion** have outstanding ball control to the degree that he was capable of carrying a heavy ball on his head before dropping it to his feet and passing with deadly accuracy, but also, when in a scoring position, he could place the ball in the net with unique precision."
Clive Dean, Tollesby, Middlesbrough.

"**Wilf Mannion** was locally born and gifted. I saw him first play in the then Teesside League at Lingdale and there were scouts everywhere, all after his signature. He could practically make the ball talk."
Mr J. E. Knight, Fulford, York.

"**George Camsell** served the Boro for 40 years and scored an incredible amount of goals. We could do with him now!"
James Henry, Middlesbrough.

"The best finisher I had the privilege to see play for Boro was **Brian Clough**. One goal from Cloughie was worth the entrance fee."
David Simpson, South Stanway, Colchester.

"**Stuart Boam** - Boro hard man, good captain, strong half-back; he could take out two attackers with one move! He always had time for the fans - he was my first autograph!"
David Shepherd, Redcar.

MY TOP 5
Harry Fawcett
Middlesbrough

1. Graeme Souness
2. Juninho
3. Bernie Slaven
4. Willie Maddren
5. John Hendrie

How about that then! The love affair between Juninho and the fans began on his debut when his skills set up a goal for Jan Fjortoft. Here, he celebrates the goal in that 1-1 draw with Leeds United.

"**Juninho** has everything a perfect player needs - skill, pace, vision and, above all, a perfect temperament on the pitch. He is the ideal player for a boy to look up to and try to emulate."
Frank Ainsworth, Eston.

"When **Juninho** is on his game, there is no-one better to rip the opposition to pieces."
Stuart Lochrie, Ormesby.

*"**Juninho's** the most naturally gifted player I have ever seen - a genius."*
Patrick McConville, Hartlepool.

*"**Juninho** has so much passion and pride in his game. He can take the ball round any defence and score goals worthy of Pele. He's a Brazilian gem."*
David Gilholm, Ardington, Oxfordshire.

"Not only is **Juninho** the most exciting player I have ever seen play for the Boro, he is the most exciting player I have ever seen!"
Mr R. W. Smith, Kingston-upon-Hull.

"During the 1996 close-season a friend of mine tried to convince me Boro should sell ***Juninho*** if we could get our money back on him. I told him he was crazy. For some reason, he no longer wants to sell him! The guy's an absolute football genius."
**Dave Allan,
MFC, PR Manager.**

*"**David Mills** was always under-rated by fans and press but he always worked hard and made defence-splitting passes, even if other Boro players were sometimes too slow to get on the end of them. He also scored a lot more goals than people realise."*
Patrick Murray, Stainton View.

Jan the Man: Fjortoft holds off a challenge from a Coventry defender during a 2-1 home victory over the Sky Blues in September 1995.

"**Souness** was the most complete player with control, speed, toughness in the tackle, a great shot, strength of mind and the will to win. He was the fulcrum of one of our most successful periods."
**Phil Dent,
Linthorpe.**

"**Wilf Mannion** had all the skills, dribbling, body swerve and also got his share of goals. I was 10 years old when I first saw him playing against Bolton and have never forgotten that game. He was a perfectionist."
Mr P. N. Byers, Guisborough.

"Having watched Middlesbrough for approximately 60 years, I still remember the skills of players of the past best and **Wilf Mannion** was the best."
Mr G. H. Fisher, Eston.

"**Juninho** is the first genuine world class player to come to Boro whilst still young enough to improve his game."
Terry French, Eston.

"Time after time, **Bernie Slaven** would win Boro the game or contribute towards a win or a draw. He was so cool in front of goal and was proud to play for the club and supporters."
Brian Mohan, Allesley, Coventry.

"**Souness** was a homesick boy going nowhere until he joined Boro and went on to be a world class player."
Richard Lyth, Hinderwell.

"**Tony Mowbray** was a very dedicated player for Boro. He was a brilliant captain and having 10 years at Boro, he didn't get his nicknames for nothing - Captain Marvel, Mr Middlesbrough, not forgetting Mogga."
Craig Close, Middlesbrough.

"**Willie Maddren** always gave 110 per cent and would be worth millions in today's market. He would also walk into today's England team."
Mr D. Pennock, Great Ayton.

"**Juninho** is a world class player and his loyalty has never been in question. He deserves the keys to the town when his contract finishes."
Colin Day, Acklam, Middlesbrough.

"**Graeme Souness** was a bargain buy for Middlesbrough Football Club, one of the all-time great midfielders who could tackle and score goals."
Kenneth Evans, Spencerbeck, Middlesbrough.

MY TOP 5
Simon Close
Eaglescliffe

1 Tony Mowbray
2 Juninho
3 Curtis Fleming
4 Heine Otto
5 Stephen Pears

Legend: goalkeeper Tim Williamson played more games for Boro than any other player - and is still fondly remembered by many long-time supporters.

"**Juninho** has made MFC recognised throughout the world because of who he is and his nationality. I have never seen his skill, determination and vision matched in any other player in the world. For me he is one of the world's best, never mind Boro's."
Martyn Stott, Bishopsgarth, Stockton.

*"**Emerson** is the most complete player I have ever seen and it is only a matter of time before he is called up for Brazil."*
Graeme Addison, Darlington.

"His 156 lbs of completely trained football genius, his educated feet and ice-box brain made **Wilf Mannion** the king of inside-forwards."
Mr A. Day, Thornaby.

"**John Hendrie** was a great goalscorer for Boro who was always 100 per cent committed to the club. He was a consistent performer and even stayed at the club for the 1995/96 season despite being only a squad player."
Simon Masri, Marton.

"**Juninho** has superb skills, balance, a heart as big as a lion, gives 100 per cent effort in every game; he is in fact a model professional footballer. My biggest compliment would be to tell young players to base their game on his commitment."
John Allison, Fairfield, Stockton.

Left-sided midfielder David Armstrong, nicknamed 'Spike', was a top choice by fans and players alike.

*"**David Armstrong** was a manager's dream - attacker, midfielder, defender rolled into one. He was also Boro's longest consecutive league games player, fantastic for a skilful, tireless worker."*

Malcolm Pearson, Middlesbrough.

Graeme Souness, the players' top choice, finished fourth in the fans' vote.

"Pound for pound, **John Hickton** is Boro's best buy. He never gave less than 100 per cent and scored many memorable and important goals."
Shaun Peacock, Fishburn.

When **Juninho** has the ball you can feel the spark of excitement run through the crowd. He has the air of greatness, elegance, grace and skill. He has great diplomacy on and off the field and to me is the true professional."
Steve Vallely, Marton Grove, Middlesbrough

"**Willie Maddren** was a player of great character, intelligence, athleticism and the best and cleanest winner of the ball I've ever seen."
Mr R. W. Gibbs, Great Ayton.

"**Juninho** shows great skill which has been lacking just a little bit in the English game. He has obviously worked and trained with a ball on his skills and techniques since he was very young."
Jill Atkinson, MFC tour guide.

*"**Tony Mowbray** was strong, committed and Boro through and through. He was a great captain and organiser at the heart of our best defensive unit for years."*
Andrew Johnston, Brighouse.

"I have no recollection of seeing Wilf Mannion so I cannot comment, but from what I have heard the little fella **Juninho** has the same qualities, skill, touch, vision, balance, determination and passion and has given MFC international credibility."
Dave Stott, Hemlington.

"**Juninho** is a diminutive football magician with more tricks up his sleeve than Paul Daniels wearing King Kong's smoking jacket."
Andrew Hogg, Ingleby Barwick.

"**Bernie Slaven** chose to stay with the club through bad times and became one of the leading all-time goalscorers. He also remains a supporter to this day."
David Carter, Middlesbrough.

"**Juninho** is everything a football genius should be. His speed, skill and determination along with his loyalty, make him the best player ever to wear a Boro shirt."
Kenny Blair, Ormesby, Middlesbrough.

"**Juninho** is the most skilful and exciting player I've seen for the Boro. He's also the man who started the Riverside revolution and gives everything for the club."
Michael Crawshaw, Billingham

"**Craig Hignett** gets a ball which people can't use and turns it into the net with great skill-plus he's a good lad with a great personality."
Kate Newton, Whitby.

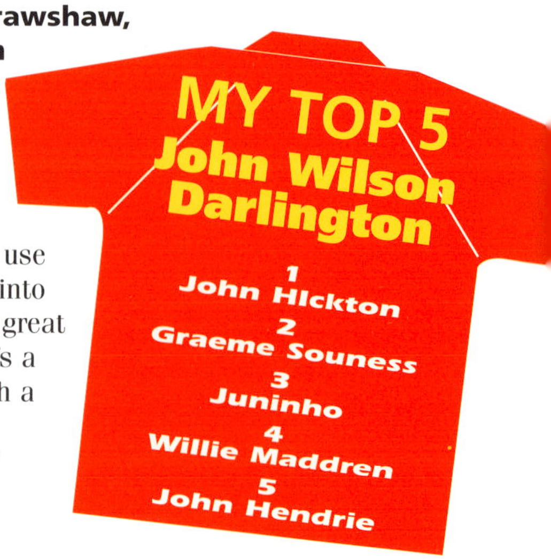

"It took a while for the signing of **Juninho** to sink in. I have never seen anyone in my years of watching the Boro, so skilful, fast or tormenting. This and the fact that he turned down bigger clubs to go to Boro, makes him my number one."
Stuart Loughran, Old Basford, Nottingham.

John Hickton was hard, fast and Boro through and through. This blond Boro Viking saw us back from oblivion to near the top again."
Derek Agar, Normanby

"My first choice is **Juninho** because the man is a genius. He plays every game with skill, honesty and passion, he plays with his heart on his sleeve and excites the crowd every time he gets the ball. Juninho wears the red of Boro with as much pride as the yellow of Brazil. He's true class, one of the best players in the world."
Gordon Rees, Linthorpe.

"**Wilf Mannion** had the ability to have most defenders kicking at fresh air. He also had the ability to pass and to get as high as most defenders in the air."
George Foster, Thorntree, Middlesbrough.

*"**John Hendrie** was the Scottish Juninho. He scored one of the greatest goals I have ever seen against Millwall. He was great on the ball, an excellent goalscorer and a great play-maker. He always played his heart out for the team and the fans and I was sorry to see him go."*
Mr R. K. Dhand, Middlesbrough.

MY TOP 5
Carlo Serino Windemere

1. Wilf Mannion
2. Tony Mowbray
3. Bernie Slaven
4. Jim Platt
5. Stuart Boam

Celebration time: two present day fans' heroes, Craig Hignett (left) and Steve Vickers (right), hold aloft the 1995 Football League championship trophy.

CELEBRITY TOP FIVES

BOB MORTIMER
Comedian

1 Juninho
2 John Craggs
3 Craig Johnston
4 Terry Cochrane
5 Jim Platt

MARK PAGE
Radio and TV personality

1 John Hickton
2 Graeme Souness
3 Bernie Slaven
4 Gary Pallister
5 Willie Maddren

ROBERT NICHOLS
editor Fly Me To The Moon

1 John Hickton
2 Bosco Jankovic
3 Juninho
4 Stephen Pears
5 Bernie Slaven

HARRY PEARSON
Author and Columnist

1 Juninho
2 Graeme Souness
3 Willie Maddren
4 Tony Mowbray
5 Bobby Murdoch

DAVID GEDDIS
MFC youth team coach

1 Bernie Slaven
2 Graeme Souness
3 John Hendrie
4 David Armstrong
5 Stuart Ripley

GORDON COX
TFM Boro commentator

1 John Hickton
2 Juninho
3 Stephen Pears
4 Bobby Murdoch
5 Eric McMordie

ANDREW SHIELDS
Sports Editor Time Out

1 John Hickton
2 Tony Mowbray
3 Jim Platt
4 David Armstrong
5 Bernie Slaven

JEFF WINTER
Premier League referee

1 Tony Mowbray
2 Willie Maddren
3 John Hickton
4 Bernie Slaven
5 Juninho

RAY TRAIN
MFC chief scout

1 Graeme Souness
2 Willie Maddren
3 Cyril Knowles
4 Tony Mowbray
5 Bobby Murdoch

PAT PARTRIDGE
Former referee

1 Wilf Mannion
2 George Hardwick
3 Bill Harris
4 Emerson
5 Brian Clough

ALAN KEEN
M.P.

1 Wilf Mannion
2 George Hardwick
3 Juninho
4 Graeme Souness
5 John Hickton

RON BONE
MFC youth dev. officer

1 Wilf Mannion
2 Brian Clough
3 George Hardwick
4 Juninho
5 Graeme Souness

MIKE McGEARY
Riverside Red columnist

1 Bernie Slaven
2 Juninho
3 Terry Cochrame
4 Tony Mowbray
5 Curtis Fleming

PETER KIRKLEY
MFC youth development

1 John Hickton
2 Brian Clough
3 Charlie Wayman
4 Lindy Delapenha
5 Juninho

GORDON McQUEEN
MFC reserve team coach

1 Graeme Souness
2 Juninho
3 Bobby Murdoch
4 Fabrizio Ravanelli
5 David Armstrong

A selection of
FANS' TOP FIVES

1 Juninho
2 Bernie Slaven
3 Tony Mowbray
4 John Hendrie
5 Curtis Fleming
Phil Ray, High Shincliffe, Durham.

1 Wilf Mannion
2 George Hardwick
3 George Camsell
4 Tim Williamson
5 Juninho
Mr V. Regan, Ormesby.

1 Juninho
2 Brian Clough
3 Graeme Souness
4 Willie Maddren
5 Emerson
Mr C. Clennan, Hinderwell.

1 Bernie Slaven
2 Juninho
3 Craig Johnston
4 John Craggs
5 Terry Cochrane
Kevin Towse, Normanby.

1 Juninho
2 Wilf Mannion
3 Brian Clough
4 John Hickton
5 John Hendrie
Paul Thompson, Guisborough.

1 Juninho
2 Graeme Souness
3 John O'Rourke
4 John Hickton
5 Bernie Slaven
Mr E. N. Bowe, Acklam.

1 Wilf Mannion
2 George Hardwick
3 Bernie Slaven
4 Willie Maddren
5 Juninho
Brian Mackin, Normanby.

1 Bernie Slaven
2 John Hendrie
3 Tony Mowbray
4 Stephen Pears
5 Paul Wilkinson
Gemma Bell, Stockton.

1 Juninho
2 John Hickton
3 Graeme Souness
4 Willie Maddren
5 Heine Otto
Stuart McLean, Leeds.

1 Juninho
2 John Hendrie
3 Heine Otto
4 John Hickton
5 Stuart Boam
Trevor Williams, Normanby.

1 Juninho
2 Fabrizio Ravanelli
3 Emerson
4 Mikkel Beck
5 Curtis Fleming
Paul Jackson, Saltburn.

1 Juninho
2 Bernie Slaven
3 John Hendrie
4 Tony Mowbray
5 Johnny Spuhler
Graeme Austick, Trimdon Village.

1 Juninho
2 Bernie Slaven
3 Emerson
4 John Hendrie
5 Gary Pallister
Adam Blacklock, Linthorpe.

1 Juninho
2 Fabrizio Ravanelli
3 Curtis Fleming
4 Robbie Mustoe
5 Phil Stamp
Stephen Bigham, Redcar.

1 Juninho
2 Emerson
3 Fabrizio Ravanelli
4 Graeme Souness
5 David Armstrong
Eddie Moir, Chorley, Lancs.

1 Wilf Mannion
2 George Hardwick
3 George Camsell
4 Brian Clough
5 Juninho
Ian Thomas Colclough, Guisborough.

MY TOP 5
Neil Shearer
Whitby
1 Bernie Slaven
2 Tony Mowbray
3 Stuart Ripley
4 Paul Wilkinson
5 John Hendrie

Another Bunch of Fives

1 Juninho
2 John Hendrie
3 Bernie Slaven
4 Bryan Robson
5 Curtis Fleming
Christopher Evans, Ormesby.

1 Wilf Mannion
2 Juninho
3 Bernie Slaven
4 Tony Mowbray
5 Gary Pallister
Mrs A. Ovington, Saltersgill.

1 Juninho
2 Bernie Slaven
3 Wilf Mannion
4 Gary Pallister
5 George Camsell
Paul Swash, Coulby Newham.

1 Tony Mowbray
2 Ian Ironside
3 Stephen Pears
4 Robbie Mustoe
5 Craig Hignett
Sarah Stevenson, Longlands.

1 Juninho
2 Graeme Souness
3 Tony Mowbray
4 John Hendrie
5 Willie Maddren
Glenn Evans, Ormesby

1 Bernie Slaven
2 Juninho
3 Tony Mowbray
4 Curtis Fleming
5 Derek Whyte
Danny Gallagher, Marton.

1 John Hickton
2 Bernie Slaven
3 Wilf Mannion
4 Juninho
5 John Hendrie
Chris Blowes, Wiggington, York.

1 Juninho
2 Stephen Pears
3 Fabrizio Ravanelli
4 John Hendrie
5 Emerson
Matthew Leach, Ipswich.

1 John Hendrie
2 Juninho
3 Gary Pallister
4 Emerson
5 Stuart Ripley
Kenneth Grange, Thorntree.

1 Juninho
2 Graeme Souness
3 Willie Maddren
4 John Hickton
5 David Armstrong
Phil Beckley, Brambles Farm.

1 Juninho
2 Fabrizio Ravanelli
3 Emerson
4 Bryan Robson
5 Uwe Fuchs
Matthew Allan, Thornaby.

1 Wilf Mannion
2 Brian Clough
3 George Hardwick
4 Bill Harris
5 Graeme Souness
Donald Love, Billingham.

1 Juninho
2 Bernie Slaven
3 Gary Pallister
4 John Hendrie
5 Stuart Ripley
Shaun Murray, Stainton View.

1 Juninho
2 John Hickton
3 George Smith
4 Bosco Jankovic
5 Craig Johnston
Fenella Pearson, Northampton.

1 Bernie Slaven
2 Willie Maddren
3 John Hendrie
4 Bryan Robson
5 Graeme Souness
John Cimmerman, Acklam.

1 Bernie Slaven
2 Juninho
3 Stephen Pears
4 David Armstrong
5 Emerson
Roger Clews, Southgate, London.

1 Juninho
2 Wilf Mannion
3 Emerson
4 Brian Clough
5 Graeme Souness
Keith Watson, Thornaby.

1 Fabrizio Ravanelli
2 John Hendrie
3 Craig Hignett
4 Graeme Souness
5 Jim Platt
David Nicholson, Rothbury.

1 Juninho
2 George Camsell
3 George Hardwick
4 Gary Pallister
5 Wilf Mannion
Gareth Hurndall, Coulby Newham.

1 Juninho
2 John Hendrie
3 Craig Hignett
4 Stephen Pears
5 Bernie Slaven
Geoff Laidlaw, Catterick Garrison.

1 Juninho
2 Curtis Fleming
3 Emerson
4 Craig Hignett
5 Robbie Mustoe
Timothy Jennings, Hemlington.

1 Juninho
2 Bernie Slaven
3 Wilf Mannion
4 John Hickton
5 Tony Mowbray
Anthony Mann, South Bank.

1 Bernie Slaven
2 Gary Pallister
3 John Hendrie
4 Juninho
5 Fabrizio Ravanelli
Steven Reed, Teesville East.

1 John Hickton
2 Willie Maddren
3 Stuart Boam
4 Tony Mowbray
5 Juninho
Kelly Morte, Park End.

1 Juninho
2 John Hickton
3 Bernie Slaven
4 Graeme Souness
5 Willie Maddren
Mr W. Thomas, Ormesby.

1 Juninho
2 Gary Pallister
3 Terry Cochrane
4 Bernie Slaven
5 John Hendrie
Neil Hamilton, Acklam.

1 Wilf Mannion
2 George Hardwick
3 Brian Clough
4 Alex McCrae
5 John Hickton
Mr E. W. Stephens, Eston.

1 Juninho
2 Wilf Mannion
3 Graeme Souness
4 Brian Clough
5 Fabrizio Ravanelli
Mr K. Gott, Linthorpe.

1 Brian Clough
2 Bill Harris
3 Willie Maddren
4 Graeme Souness
5 Juninho
Mr R. A. Peel, Marske.

1 Brian Clough
2 Graeme Souness
3 Wilf Mannion
4 John O'Rourke
5 Bernie Slaven
Mr G. Tranter, Teesville East.

MY TOP 5
Mrs M. Breckon
Eaglescliffe
1
Brian Clough
2
Bernie Slaven
3
Alan Peacock
4
Arthur Kaye
5
Juninho

1 Rolando Ugolini
2 Lindy Delapenha
3 Micky Fenton
4 Bill Linacre
5 Craig Johnston
Peter Gallagher, Boroughbridge.

1 John Hendrie
2 Juninho
3 Wilf Mannion
4 Curtis Fleming
5 Bernie Slaven
David & Pauline Coombes, Eaglescliffe.

1 Brian Clough
2 Graeme Souness
3 Tony Mowbray
4 Wilf Mannion
5 Bernie Slaven
David McConnell, Thatcham, Berkshire.

1 Wilf Mannion
2 John O'Rourke
3 John Hickton
4 Graeme Souness
5 Stephen Pears
Paul Edward Fionda, Linthorpe.

"**Wilf Mannion** was a world class player with outstanding ability - dribbling, passing, shooting, heading. In an era of many great players, he stood out as a superstar."
Mr C. Graye, Boston Spa, Wetherby.

"I have never seen a more skilful player than **Juninho**. He can change a game in a second and never complains. I can't remember him having a bad game for the club."
Mr K. Beckett, Redcar.

"**Juninho** is a truly remarkable, gifted player and a loyal and honest man, in fact, a giant of a man. We adore him."
Josephine Jones, Redcar.

"**Wilf Mannion** was the most gifted player I have seen. Sadly, the war years interrupted his career when it would have been at its best."
Mr J. T. Marshall, Nunthorpe.

"**Juninho** is the very best - very skilful, very quick, very cheeky and very cute!"
Hazel Day, Stockton.

*"**Tony Mowbray** was a local lad who gave his all and was proud to be captain of his home-town club."*
Douglas Mortlock, Fairfield, Stockton.

"Defenders are terrified when **Juninho** runs at them at terrific speed and his control of the ball is excellent. He's on a different level to some players."
Mr A. Archer, Normanby.

"I would say **Wilf Mannion** were the nearest thing to the complete forward. He must have been a nightmare for opposing defenders."
Mr M. E. Brunton, Aycliffe Village, County Durham.

"**Juninho** is the most gifted and exhilarating player I have ever seen. His attitude is exemplary. Even when the team plays badly, he always wants the ball and he lets his football on the pitch do the talking."
Andy Emmerson, Bilton Rugby, Cumbria.

"For all-round ability it has to be **Wilf Mannion**. He was two-footed, a brilliant header of the ball and perfectly balanced."
Harry Antill, Skelton.

He may have played his last game for the club more than 60 years ago but the memory of Jackie Carr still burns bright for older Boro supporters.

"**Juninho** is like a magic wand - when he waves it we win the games. He is hungry to succeed at Boro and is a model professional."
Mr S. D. Whittingham, Acklam.

*"**David Hodgson** was a player who wore his heart on his sleeve. He always gave 100 per cent commitment and determination and never gave up chasing for what others considered lost causes. He was a player fans could relate to."*
John Taylor, Brooklands, Manchester.

"I saw **Wilf Mannion** for the first time in my early teens when I was amazed at his skill with the ball. He was magic to watch and remains my all-time favourite."
Beryl Thomas, Thornaby.

"Not only is **Juninho** a brilliant, skilful player but most importantly, his heart is really with the Boro which is excellent to see from a foreign star. The Riverside certainly comes alive when he is playing."
Nicholas Henegan, Acklam.

"**John Hickton** was my childhood hero who knew what to do - score goals, and always gave 110 per cent."
Graham Palmer, Nunthorpe.

"The little man **Juninho** is head and shoulders above everyone else."
Mr M. Monkhouse, Stockton.

*"**Willie Maddren** was the best uncapped player of his era and was also a great player and sportsman."*
Paul Tucker, Linthorpe.

*"**Bernie Slaven** only needed a sniff of a chance and he was there like a bloodhound."*
Peter Ashley Johnson, Port Clarence.

"As a boy, **Wilf Mannion's** magic started me on a life-time's love of football. On his day, no other player world-wide and through the years could even approach him."
Jim Thompson, Coulby Newham.

"No matter how many players and memorable times I remember at the Boro, one always comes to mind - St Valentine's Day 1988, a marvellous diving header to beat the Villa from **Tony Mowbray**, a captain who was Boro through and through."
David Buck, Whitby.

"With his never-say-die attitude and cracking goal tally, **John Hickton** epitomised Middlesbrough FC. He was a true professional."
John Brookes, Hartburn.

Paul Wilkinson celebrates one of two goals in an unforgettable 4-1 victory over reigning champions Leeds United in 1992. Such goals made Wilko a huge favourite on the Ayresome Park terraces.

Paul Wilkinson holds the record for making the most Boro first team appearances in one season. Wilko played 60 times for the club in 1991-92 - 46 in the league, eight in the Rumbelows Cup, four in the FA Cup and two in the ZDS Cup.

A number of fans picked right-back Neil Cox - in action against Coventry's Darren Huckerby - in their all-time top five.

"I voted for ***Craig Hignett*** *as my number one because he took a wage cut to stay with Boro even though he's not a local lad or supports them - that's commitment. He's also a good all-round player."*
Lucy Hosking,
Ben Rhydding, Ilkley.

"**Juninho** has the ability to ghost past world class defenders and actually does it regularly. He can change a game with his runs and direct style which is what the fans like to see and he entertains the fans. He usually seems to have so much time on the ball and is great in tight spaces. His control of the ball is amazing with a good first touch."
Paul Norminton, Ferryhill.

"**Brian Clough** was a class striker in an otherwise average side. His scoring record spoke for itself."
Mr J. Carter, Hemlington.

Goal ace Fabrizio Ravanelli celebrates Boro's first in a 2-2 Premiership draw with champions Manchester United in November 1996.

By the end of the 1996/97 campaign Robbie Mustoe – seen here battling through the Liverpool defence during a 3-3 opening day draw – was Boro's longest-serving player. His loyalty and footballing brain made him one of the club's most popular stars.

"With all the big money players that have come and gone from the club, **Robbie Mustoe** has just got on with it and always grafted away for the team and the club. He has never been any trouble to any of the managers but at the same time is mixing it with some of the best players in the world. Robbie is without doubt the Boro's unsung hero."
Derek Weaver, Teesville, Middlesbrough.

"**Juninho's** playing skills rank among the best in the world and his dedication both on and off the pitch are simply outstanding. He is one in a million!"
James Swales, Thirsk.

*"**John Hendrie** was an exciting player who always gave 100 per cent and scored the best goal I have ever seen in 30 years of watching Boro."*
Mr J. Smithard, Yarm.

"It's great to see the best player in the world, **Juninho**, play in a Boro shirt."
Ian Taylor, Linthorpe.

"**Juninho** gives 100 per cent effort, he's got speed, skill and stamina, plus a footballing brain others dream of."
Colin Harston, Stockton.

"**Wilf Mannion** had a marvellous sense of anticipation, ball control and a body swerve which was out of this world."
Mr K. R. Fox, Acklam.

"**Juninho** is the most skilful player I have ever seen but also he never gives up, tries 100 per cent and plays with pride."
Mr P. S. Stephenson, Hartlepool.

*"**Fabrizio Ravanelli** has an aura of class unseen before in Middlesbrough."*
Michael Chubb, Acklam.

"**Wilf Mannion** was the most complete player and always gave his best. I remember the Blackpool match many years ago when Mannion was outstanding. Both sets of players gave him a standing ovation."
Mr F. R. Bingham, Stainton.

*"**Bobby Murdoch** changed a reasonable Second Division team into a strong First Division team."*
Mr C. J. Davey, Billingham.

"**Bernie Slaven** scored many crucial goals, particularly away from home. He got us to our first Wembley final and was crucial to our various promotion campaigns."
Graham Thompson, Yarm.

"**Juninho** is the most skilful player I have ever seen in a Boro shirt and a real gentleman. He's a credit to his country and club."
Mr D. A. Twigg, Redcar.

"**Juninho** is a genuine world class talent and would fit into any world club side. He also has a committed attitude to Boro's cause."
Mr P. Hughes, Macclesfield, Cheshire.

"Although **Tony Mowbray** may not have been the most skilful player to play for the Boro, he gave everything he ever had and more, playing every game - whether at Manchester United or Mansfield Town - as if it was his last. A more committed, honest and brave player in a Boro shirt, you will never see."
Geoff Thomas, Thornaby.

*"In my opinion, **Stephen Pears** was often the unsung hero of many games, an excellent goalkeeper."*
Michael Bashford, Saltburn.

Bryan Robson made a playing comeback at Highbury on New Year's Day 1997 just a few days short of his 40th birthday.

Overseas signings Emerson (left) and Mikkel Beck made immediate impacts at the Cellnet Riverside Stadium during 1996-97.

Boro fans enjoyed the goalscoring ability of Micky Fenton either side of the Second World War.

"**Juninho** is the most skilful player I've seen in 40 years watching the Boro. He can turn defenders inside out. He's surely destined to be one of the world's best."
Mr A. Haverson, Swadlincote, Derbyshire.

*"**John Hickton's** my number one for his prolific and consistent goalscoring record and loyal service shown over many years."*
Paul Watson, Fairfield, Stockton.

MY TOP 5
Kenneth Grange
Thorntree

1. John Hendrie
2. Juninho
3. Gary Pallister
4. Emerson
5. Stuart Ripley

"**Juninho** has settled in and shows why Brazil are light years ahead of England."
Mr D. Palmer, Egglescliffe.

MY TOP 5
Peter Gallagher
Boroughbridge

1. Rolando Ugolini
2. Lindy Delapenha
3. Micky Fenton
4. Bill Linacre
5. Craig Johnston

"**Juninho** is the best player I have ever seen anywhere in the world. we are truly privileged to have him grace our stadium and team."
Sarah Walker, Redcar

*"**Tony Mowbray** was 100 per cent committed to the Boro, a local lad made good and a fine example to Boro youngsters."*
Dave Barton, York.

"If I don't vote for God - **Bernie Slaven** - he may strike me down!"
Steven Secker, Grangefield, Stockton.

"Pound for pound, **Juninho** is Boro's greatest asset. The waif-like genius is blessed with skill, the right temperament and the ability to control games."
Anthony McNicholas, Eston

"**Brian Clough** had an unerring ability to score exciting goals profusely."
Derek Johnstone, Marton

*"Having watched Boro from 1932 and still being a season ticket holder, I have seen them all. Forwards always seem to get all the praise hence **Wilf Mannion** is my number one before George Hardwick - but only just."*
Mr J. Richardson, Teesville, Middlesbrough.

Curtis Fleming's sterling service and outstanding performances have earned him Irish caps and a place in the hearts of Boro fans.

"**Juninho** is a superbly skilful and gifted player with pace and an ability to score great goals. He's tremendous."
Garry Charlton, Spennymoor.

"The moment **Alan Foggon** rolled his socks down you knew there would be some action."
Valerie Bell, Stockton.

"**Juninho** symbolises the new Boro - skilful, sporting and world class."
Mr C. Terry, Saltburn.

*"**Wilf Mannion** had great ball control and good vision. He was a great creative player, a good passer of the ball and could score goals with either foot."*
Neil O'Donnell, Marton.

"**Graeme Souness** never gave less than 100 per cent and always won his battles in midfield. He had a great shot and was a superb passer."
Mr S. Thomas, Thornaby.

The Golden Boy scores against Sheffield Wednesday in 1953. Wilf Mannion won many votes from both fans and players.

Derek Whyte's resolute defending over five years helped him pick up a number of fans' votes.

One of the best: Tony Mowbray enjoyed a great rapport with the supporters throughout his years with the club. Here, he waves farewell to them during his final game for the Boro.

Further fans' favourites included:

Nigel PEARSON, Eric McMORDIE, Johnny SPUHLER, Ian GIBSON, Jim IRVINE, Don MASSON, Rolando UGOLINI, Jackie CARR, Derek WHYTE, George ELLIOT, Ian IRONSIDE, Mel NURSE, Gary HAMILTON, Alan PEACOCK, George SMITH, Archie STEPHENS, Charlie WAYMAN, Neil COX, Dean GLOVER, Bosco JANKOVIC, Arthur KAYE, Bill LINACRE, Tony McANDREW, Alex McCRAE, Alan MOORE, Dicky ROBINSON, Willie WHIGHAM , Gary WALSH, Bob BRAITHWAITE, Mark BURKE, Willie FERNIE, William FORREST, Vladimir KINDER, Andy PAYTON, Jamie POLLOCK, Ben ROBERTS, Dicky ROOKS, Phil STAMP, Harry BELL, Ronnie DICKS, Jack JENNINGS, Arthur FITZSIMMONS.

"**Juninho** has brought a lot of charisma to the club, gives over 100 per cent effort and has been no trouble to the club."
Mrs J. Bartley, Stokesley.

"The sight of **Big John Hickton** running with the ball, and those penalties - marvellous!"
Brian Desmond, Ormesby.

"**Juninho's** skills and commitment to the club are fabulous. He's probably the best player to play for Boro. Brazil-iant!"
Martin McDonald, Saltburn.

"In a career cruelly cut short by injury, **Willie Maddren's** skill, courage and determination together with his partnership with Boam, gave us the best defensive play I'ver ever seen from a Boro team."
Mr M. J. Stone, Thornaby.

*"After the crisis of liquidation, a character on and off the field such as **Bernie Slaven** was needed. He proved himself to the vast majority of Boro fans and has a place in my heart forever."*
Greg Stinson, Newton, Middlesbrough.

*"**David Hodgson's** my number one for his attitude to win on the field, his speed on the wing and his close rapport with the fans."*
Paul English, Billingham.

"**Wilf Mannion** had all-round ability - ball skills, heading ability - basically, the perfect goal-scoring midfield player."
Mr P. P. Banks, Redcar.

"**Juninho** has great ability and attitude. He gives everything asked of him and more."
Paul Dodds, Middleton St George.

"**Juninho's** skills are equal to Wilf Mannion's but are displayed every game. His penetrating runs are wonderful. But, admire him as I do, he has a long way to go to match Mannions famous display against Blackpool."
Mr. J. D. Allan, Middlesbrough.

Bernie Slaven was second only to Juninho in the affections of Boro supporters.